No New Ideas

Everything You Need to Know
About Starting a Successful Franchise

By Tim Conn, CFE

ISBN-13: 978-1-7338532-3-1   Paperback

ISBN-13: 978-1-7338532-4-8   eBook

Dedication

To Maria, my wonderful wife who has always believed in me and supported me through all my decisions, good or bad.

To our children, Anthony and Nikko, who have been a part of the business since before they could walk! There is nothing more satisfying than seeing your success in business and life.

To my parents, thank you for teaching me about business from a very young age. I wish you could be here to see the success that has resulted from your guidance.

Praise for *No New Ideas*

"Tim Conn sheds light on a business most people interact with on a daily basis but few understand and his book is packed with details that only someone who's been in the trenches would know. *No New Ideas* should be considered required reading for anyone considering entering the franchise world." – Jody Williamson, Managing Director, Sandler Training Chicago/Northbrook

"In *No New Ideas*, Tim Conn shares his knowledge of franchising to both advise and encourage those looking to go into business for themselves. His candor is refreshing—he reminds the reader constantly that hard work and countless sacrifices go into owning your own business—but he also illustrates, brilliantly, how the 'Return on You' makes it all worthwhile." – Mark Siebert, CEO of The iFranchise Group, author of *Franchise Your Business: The Guide to Employing the Greatest Growth Strategy Ever*

"*No New Ideas* is a highly enjoyable and thought-provoking read for anyone contemplating franchise ownership. Tim Conn shares his real-life experiences in ways that truly engage the reader to perfectly illustrate the many realities of business ownership." – Linda Menter, Vice President of Business Development, FranChoice Inc.

"A must-read book for anyone considering franchising. Tim Conn is one of the very few people that can both do and teach. His real-world knowledge of franchising from both perspectives—as a franchisee and franchisor—are priceless. *No New Ideas* is packed with information that most franchisees never find out until it's too late."
– Joel Weldon, Hall of Fame speaker and creator of the Ultimate Speaking System

For more information about franchises, visit www.TimsFranchiseBook.com.

Table of Contents

Introduction

Over the holidays this year, we had close friends come to stay with us in Florida. My friend's son, who recently graduated college, was getting ready to go on his first corporate job interview in Colorado. Over dinner, the young man was asking us all how he should prepare.

"What about you, Tim?" he asked. "What do you do before a job interview?"

I laughed and said, "I haven't been on a single job interview in my life so I'm probably not the person to ask."

I might have been laughing, but I wasn't joking. I have owned and operated my own business since I was 10 years old, starting with my first lawn mowing job when I offered $10 landscaping services to any neighbor willing to trust a kid with a lawnmower. When fall came, I raked the neighbors' leaves, and as our seasons changed to winter in Chicago, I grabbed a shovel from the garage and walked door to door helping friends and neighbors (for a fee of course)!

I think even from a young age, I knew the W-2 life just wasn't for me. It's not that I didn't want to work—quite the opposite. Owning your own business means you are never off the clock. I loved working. But what I loved even more was having the opportunity to create the schedule around which I worked. It wasn't that I didn't or couldn't follow rules, although my teachers might have disagreed. I simply preferred to manage other people, rather than being managed myself. I liked being my own boss.

I am going to guess that you do too, which is probably why you're reading this book.

My goal is to help you succeed. Maybe you'll decide you're interested in janitorial services, but that's not my objective.

If you've ever had the crazy idea of starting your own business, or the desire to be self-employed, if you've ever dreamed of doing your own thing, but you just didn't know how or what you wanted to do, if you're trying to figure out what your next step in your professional life should be, or if you're just trying to figure out "what you want to be when you grow up," then this is the book for you. And as you read through it, you can always find more information and resources at our website, www.timsfranchisebook.com.

A lot of people out there don't want to just make money for someone else. They want to build a business for themselves. But being in business for yourself isn't always easy. The reality is that many small businesses don't succeed. According to the latest data, 20% of small business fail in their first year, 50% of them fail after five years, and 70% of small business owners have failed by their 10th year of business—and that's after nearly a decade of invested time, money, and effort.

With statistics like that, entrepreneurs would probably be more likely to succeed if they had a safety net—

something to catch them when they fall, something to help them bounce back from difficult times and to offer support when they are struggling. The idea of a franchise is exactly that: a safety net to help franchisees avoid failure. While there is still no guarantee of success, a franchise system assists the business owner in avoiding challenges with which other business owners might find themselves struggling.

A safety net was something I didn't have when I started my first business. And there were times when I struggled greatly running my own business, with everything from finances to staffing to billing to just about everything else a new entrepreneur has to deal with on a regular basis. There were times when I was so frustrated I wanted to give up (which, as a business owner, is a totally normal feeling from time to time). I thought, "What am I doing? I work longer hours than anybody I know, and I have all of these headaches." It caused tension at home between me and my wife, Maria. I remember many occasions when she would say, "Why don't you just quit this stupid business and go to work for somebody else? You could make so much more money and avoid all the aggravation."

Every time she'd say that, I would get so mad that it would motivate me to go out and prove I could do it. Her criticism actually became my inspiration. It wasn't that she was trying to be negative; she simply wanted what was best for me, her, and our new family (we had two young sons at the time). Sorry, Maria!

Looking back, I realize how lucky I've been over the last 35 years. I found a business that was recession-proof, relatively quick to learn, and easy to scale: the glamorous job of janitorial services.

Sure, cleaning toilets doesn't sound like a dream job, but here's the thing: businesses might forego a lot of needs, but rarely does a business owner want to scrub his own bathroom floor. Having been in this business a long time, I have seen many changes over the years. When I started, Ronald Reagan was president, and the economy was rebounding from super-high inflation in the late 1970s and early 80s. The economy was booming, and I took a ride on the coattails of that economy. There were ups and downs over the years. Changes in which party controlled the White House and Congress. Changes across the whole world that affected various parts of my life. The one thing that remained constant? Every year my business grew.

People can complain about their circumstances, or they can do something about them. There is a common saying, "It is what it is," which implies that you're simply forced to accept something. I couldn't disagree more. I prefer a different version: **It is what you make of it.** In other words: take the situation and turn it into what you want it to be. When the economy is bad and clients are struggling to pay their invoices, I see opportunity. If somebody can't afford my competitor, I can save them some money and I can grow my business. On the other hand, if the economy is good, and businesses are growing and expanding, I can…still grow my business. Either way, it's a win.

The janitorial business gave me freedom of schedule, consistent and lucrative income, and a reliability rarely matched in the world of independent businesses.

My company sign might have said janitor, but my real job was being an entrepreneur.

Most people aren't drawn to operating a small business for the product or service, but rather for the freedom a small business provides. It's no wonder that small businesses account for so much of the American economy. According to the Census Bureau's 2016 Annual Survey of Entrepreneurs, there were 5.6 million employer firms in the United States in 2016. Firms with fewer than 100 workers accounted for 98% of those businesses, and firms with fewer than 20 workers made up 89%.

I started my first real small business at the age of 14, cleaning an office building my parents owned. My parents were business owners themselves, and I grew up seeing the upside of entrepreneurship. Sure, there were risks and rough times that maybe other families didn't face, but my parents were always able to provide for my siblings and me. We spent time together as a family, travelled more than most, and were taught that if you wanted things in life, you needed to go out and work for them. Cable came out when I was 10 years old. Though we had cable in the family room, my brother and I were told that if we wanted cable in our room, we would have to pay for the box. It was only $10 a month, split between two of us, but that was a lot of money for a couple of kids. Still, we wanted more than the three network stations in our room. That's what led me to the lawn mowing business.

Once I started cleaning my parents' office building, I realized I had struck gold. For only a couple hours of work, I could charge a substantial fee (well, substantial enough for a 14-year-old). I started going out and marketing my services, and by the time I went to college, I had launched a full-blown janitorial service company.

I operated Tidy Tim's Cleaning Service from 1985 to 2001, which is why in all those years, when my other friends were going out on job interviews and trying to get by on minimum wage, I was busy inter-viewing other people and negotiating *their* salaries and benefits.

I was cleaning office and apartment buildings while offering window washing on the side. As early as high school, I began attending networking events where I received my first major contract: cleaning a local AT&T store. Everything went so well that I was awarded several locations throughout the Chicago area. By the time I was ready to graduate college, the career counselor called me in for a meeting.

He sat across from me, disappointment on his face.

"You have good grades," he said. "You have so much potential, Tim. What I don't understand is why you haven't been preparing yourself for a career."

"What do you mean?" I asked him, confused by his concern.

"Well, you haven't been attending any of the job fairs."

I was a little embarrassed to tell him that not only did I already have a job but I actually had employees of my own. In hindsight, I realized that I should have been enrolling in one of the fairs as a vendor.

After college, I hired someone who was an expert in window washing. Together, we landed a contract with one of the big malls and expanded from there. A few years later, I was cleaning an office building that included a dialysis center. At first, I was only cleaning their office side, but they were so happy with our work that they asked if we could also manage the medical side, which led to a whole new niche of businesses.

At this point, you're probably wondering: what does all this cleaning have to do with you?

Well, I can tell you right now: everything.

Because in 2001, I had the opportunity to join the franchise industry. I received a letter from somebody who had just purchased a janitorial master franchise for the Chicago market and he wanted to see if I would be interested in running the new janitorial franchise. It would include my own businesses, and I would have the opportunity to sell the franchises to my employees. At this point, I had been running a janitorial company for over 15 years. Suddenly, I had the chance to scale my business.

The only thing was, I didn't know a thing about franchising.

Like a lot of franchisors, I never started out with franchising in mind.

But suddenly, I had an opportunity to build upon my business and help other people get into business for themselves. All the risks and rewards I experienced through my decades in the industry could be used to support other people looking for the same freedom and opportunity I had sought since I'd started out cleaning my parents' office building at the age of 14.

Since 2001, I have discovered the risks and rewards of franchising. I have seen what works, and I have watched people fail. The one thing I realized is that franchising offers a lot of the same rewards as an independent business—flexibility, entrepreneurship, and profit—without the same risks.

Unfortunately, a lot of people jump into franchising without really understanding what makes a franchise successful and what can make them a successful franchisee.

There are thousands of franchises out there—from McDonald's to insurance companies to janitorial services to fitness centers to retail galore. There are home-based services and brick-and-mortar businesses. There are ways to be successful, and there are ways not to.

At Image One USA, the janitorial franchise company I still run today, we work with our franchisees to help them build successful businesses, walking them through the process to ensure their hard work produces long-term results. Our franchisees are like family to us—we are all invested in one another's success. I hope that as you read this book, you'll feel the same way.

I want to help you find the franchise that is right for you, the company that is the best culture fit, and a system that will help you take that franchise to the next level. Over the next eight chapters, I believe we can get there.

Most people don't realize that many of the businesses they go to every day are part of a franchise. When you buy a car, have your car serviced, go to a restaurant, or hit your local gym, you are likely at a franchised establishment. When you go to a retail store to ship a package, or when you bring your kids in for tutoring after school, you are likely visiting a franchise. They are everywhere, and they are owned by people just like you who decided they wanted to be in business for themselves. As of 2018, there were over 760,000 operational franchises in the US. That is one in seven businesses. And of those establishments, there are over 3,500 franchisors, which means when you go looking to open a franchise, you have a LOT of options.

I go to probably too many franchise shows, and I can always spot when it's someone's first time. They are wide eyed and overwhelmed when they walk into the conference center. Immediately, they are swarmed by people offering them free pens and tote bags, telling them about the latest trend and the fastest way to build a successful franchise. There are hundreds of vendors, and I am sure that every opportunity is good for the right person. But every business isn't right for every person.

I hope this book is the opposite of that experience. I'm not here to overwhelm you with the latest fads or the best sales pitch.

We'll take a look at what your interests are, and we'll gauge your capabilities. We'll review what kind of franchises are out there and what level of investment (namely time, money, and energy) they demand. Then we'll walk through the process—from doing your due diligence on a company to participating in a discovery or meet-the-team day. We'll discuss Franchise Disclosure Documents and what a traditional franchise agreement looks like. Then we'll go over the strategies that work …and those that don't work.

The franchise business model supports nearly 7.6 million jobs and yields $674.3 billion of economic output. That's 2.5% of US GDP. Though economists have long disputed the "stat" that 95% of all franchises survive, recent surveys show that 91.2% of franchise businesses were still open after two years and 85% were operating after five.

One of the biggest strengths of a franchise is that you are buying a time-tested system. Someone else has already made the mistakes so you don't have to.

That's what we're going to do here. By reading this book, you won't have to make the same mistakes others have made in the past. You'll be prepared to make the best decision for yourself, your business, and your family. And you'll be equipped with the right strategies to turn that decision into a successful business.

And if you succeed? You'll never have to go on a job interview again. I promise.

Chapter One:
There Are No New Ideas

Many entrepreneurs believe the first step in business is coming up with a million-dollar idea that's never been done before.

But the truth is, every great accomplishment has its predecessor.

Elon Musk's technology for an electric car was founded in the inventions of its namesake, Nikola Tesla.

The modern internet was originally developed by scientists in the 1930s who were simply reimagining the modern library as a mechanized system.

Even man's arrival on the moon was first conceived centuries earlier by the great astronomer Galileo.

We might think we are the first on the scene but, chances are, someone else got there centuries before us.

Most modern businesses are just better developed, more perfected (we hope!) versions of someone else's idea. And that includes the concept of franchising.

Though modern franchising is often attributed to Isaac Singer, founder of the Singer sewing machine, who developed the first franchise contract in the mid-1800s in order to help him distribute his sewing machines across the country, franchising started long before him, and way before Ray Kroc opened his first McDonald's franchise in 1955.

Franchising has been around for over 1,000 years in one form or another. Even Isaac Singer and Ray Kroc were just building better developed, more perfected systems from concepts that had been hanging around for centuries.

The History of Franchising

For some of you, knowing the history of franchising is important. If that's you, keep reading; if you don't care about the history of franchising, at least skim through this section so you have an idea of where it all began.

Most people are not aware that the business model of franchising started over 1,500 years ago in the Middle Ages. Local government officials would grant rights and duties that were similar to governing to high church officials and other people.

From assessing taxes to maintaining order, these government franchises allowed the state to have more local influence on their communities. In turn, these "franchisees" were able to set up local businesses, paying a royalty for the influence.

This form of franchising continued into the colonial period, when government agencies were often many continents and a few oceans away. In order to exert control of the Crown, local Lords would give permission to people of importance to run local markets, manage ferries, and hunt on the "Lord's land." Similar to the modern franchise, "franchisees" would pay a royalty to the King for both the opportunity to hold power and protection.

This notion of protection has certainly carried over to the modern franchise, as the franchisee is not just paying for the idea or the system (though both are critical) but also for the shared risk that the franchisor holds.

In the 1840s, a German brewing company allowed local tavern owners to sell their beer and use their brand name for a payment. The tavern owners were able to utilize the beer brand, Spaten, in order to draw in more customers. Instead of using the power of the Crown to grow revenue, businesses began to use the power of a brand.

This is why in the mid-1800s, Isaac Singer, the founder and inventor of the Singer sewing machine, recognized that not only could he sell his sewing machine, but he could also sell the brand itself to others in his industry by granting them licenses to sell the Singer machine. As part of the agreement, "franchisees" would teach people how to use the sewing machine, which would in turn increase sales.

Singer's concepts came just in time, as only a few years later, another product would enter the market that would forever change the progress of mankind. In 1896, William Metzger opened the first automobile dealership in Detroit, Michigan. Automobile manufacturers recognized that they needed a way to sell their cars, and since the automobile was a new product, people needed to be able to go somewhere to see how it worked (also, many needed to learn how to drive). The automobile dealership was the perfect solution, and as car sales grew, so did the number of dealership locations. This gave auto manufacturers a network of franchises to sell their automobiles, greatly increasing their sales and brand recognition. The dealerships not only offered a strong brick-and-mortar presence in the community, but also engendered word-of-mouth marketing across the country—the best and freest kind there is.

In response to the influx of cars on the roads, gas stations began to spring up as Americans and people all over the country needed access to petroleum on a regular basis. Many of these were also franchises. And the more time people spent on the road driving, the greater the need for roadside restaurants—like a little place known for its golden arches.

In 1955, Ray Kroc opened the first McDonald's franchise in Des Plaines, Illinois, founding McDonald's System, Inc, which later became the McDonald's Corporation. Kroc bought out the McDonald brothers in 1961 for $2.7 million, expanding the restaurant to over 500 locations in only eight years, paving the way for the modern franchise. Today, there are over 34,000 McDonald's restaurants in over 109 countries.

After the advent of McDonald's, franchising boomed throughout the 1950s and 1960s, cooling in the 1970s when franchisors started failing to support their franchisees. However, franchising made a comeback in the late 1980s and early 1990s with the rise of fitness systems, health and food trends like TCBY and Subway, and the increase in at-home businesses.

Franchising Today

Currently, the number of franchise establishments in the United States is approximately 760,000, grown from 698,000 just five years before. All of these businesses employ over eight million people combined, with Quick Service Restaurants (QSR) and Table/Full-Service Restaurants accounting for approximately 50% of all jobs in the franchising industry.

Since 2000, the industry has continued to change and adapt. First, there has been an increase in multi-unit franchisees, which now control more franchises than the total of all single-unit franchisees. Since 2011, 50% of franchisee growth has been generated by existing franchisees[1]. In addition, more franchises are being consolidated under a common parent or two, which means there are fewer single-unit franchises in the market. For example, the world's 10 largest hotel chains now offer a combined 113 brands at various price points, 31 of which didn't exist a decade ago. With these changes, multi-brand franchise systems and

---

[1] Texeira, Ed. "Seismic Changes Are Altering the Franchise Industry," *Forbes*, May 25, 2018.

multi-unit franchisees continue to grow in popularity and influence, while those single-unit franchises who find it difficult to compete will likely fold. However, these changes have also created a number of new opportunities in the franchising world.

Over the last 20 years, franchising has expanded into more at-home services, information technologies, and other tech-related services. Currently, there are an estimated 3,000 different franchisors operating in the U.S. today across 300 business categories in the U.S.

According to CNBC, "Franchise establishments are set to grow by 1.9% to 759,000 locations after increasing 1.6% in 2017, while employment will increase 3.7% to 8.1 million workers after growing 3.1% in 2017. The gross domestic product of the sector is forecast to increase by 6.1% to $451 billion, and will contribute approximately 3% of U.S. GDP in nominal dollars, according to the report. Franchise business output will also increase 6.2% to $757 billion.[2]"

---

[2] Rogers, Kate. "Thanks in part to Trump's tax reform, franchise industry is set for another year of major growth," *CNBC*, January 29, 2018.

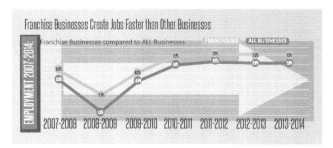

Courtesy of the International Franchise
Association (IFA) Educational Foundation, 2014.

Though the average initial investment for a franchise is $250,000, that number can be significantly higher or smaller, depending on the industry. For example, to open up a janitorial franchise with Image One, new franchisees invest less than $50,000 upfront for their franchise fee, a portion of which can be financed.

The average royalty fees paid by franchisees range from 3-10% of monthly gross sales, depending on the business and industry. The return on investment (ROI) can vary widely, depending on what kind of franchise you're investing in and, ultimately, what level of yield you anticipate. However, you should be able expect a strong return on your invested capital (according to *Entrepreneur* magazine, somewhere in the neighborhood of 15%). In other words, for every $100,000 of your capital you invest, you should anticipate making at least $15,000 per year in ROI. However, most franchises offer a greater return than that—in general, successful franchises usually offer a

20-25% return on investment, after calculating for both the active and passive investment costs[3].

It's no surprise that the franchise is growing in popularity. In 2017, the number of franchise establishments increased by 1.6% across all 10 business-format lines. Personal services industries, like childcare and fitness centers, led in growth with a 2.5% increase, followed closely by quick service restaurants at 1.8%. Similarly, franchise employment also increased to over 3%.

Most business people don't start out with franchising in mind. I certainly didn't. You start a company, and if you're successful, the next step is to scale, expanding operations to new locations or more clients. But with that growth also come challenges. As a business owner, you can't be in all places at all times, yet, if there is a market for your goods, why shouldn't you continue to grow with that demand?

What brought me into franchising was realizing that I had developed a system that could be sold to other people in order to help them grow their own businesses. I had learned the hard way over two decades of janitorial experience.

There was a clear demand for our product. By franchising, I could support other small business owners while meeting that demand with my product.

---

[3] Brecht, Kara. "Are Franchises a Good Investment?" US News and World Report, September 13, 2016.

For business owners, the choice becomes clear: either cede the market to a competitor or find ways to expand your business. By selling off franchise locations, business owners not only become franchisors but they are also able to achieve sustainable growth and meet the demands of the market.

It's no surprise more companies are turning to franchising, and it's no surprise more people are becoming franchisees.

Why Become a Franchisee?

Many people recognize that they want to run their own business but don't want to have to open one. Starting a business from the ground up is an uphill task. While operating a franchise isn't easy, you're at least going uphill using someone else's engine with a pit crew to help with problems along the way.

There are a lot of benefits to becoming a franchisee, many of which I didn't realize until I became a franchisor. Through Image One, franchisees have been able to buy their first homes, send their children to college, and build a presence in their communities simply by running and operating their own franchise. Franchising offers many of the same opportunities that were offered in the Middle Ages—the chance to become an integral part of your community, to establish a successful business, and to receive protection from a more-established partner. But there are many more benefits to becoming a franchisee. Let's take a look at a few:

- **Service**—the biggest benefit to becoming a franchisee is that you are buying a system that offers an established product or service. You do not need to invent the wheel; you don't even need to reinvent it. Franchising is a lot like the popular food delivery services Blue Apron or Hello Fresh. The ingredients and instructions are already there. When you follow them, you end up with a dish that looks like the picture. When you don't, you're left wondering whether your purchase was worth it.

- **Systems**—This is the biggest benefit (and challenge) in franchising: someone has already done the work of developing and establishing a viable business system. The franchisor has already made the mistakes and learned from them so you don't have to. It's like you get to take a head start in a race. Unfortunately, many franchisees struggle because they try to buck those systems. You are spending good money for the work others have already put in. My most successful franchisees are the ones who follow the system to the letter. It doesn't mean they don't have some great ideas, but they don't try them on their own. They come to us, and if we agree, we incorporate them into the already-established system (after all, that is what they are paying for).

- **Brand**—Whether it's on the local or international level (or somewhere in-between), the biggest product you are purchasing as a franchisee is the brand. McDonald's is disputably just a good hamburger, but the McDonald's brand is one of the most recognizable names in the world. Which do you think people are investing in? You are buying a built-in audience with the brand, one that people are familiar with and, in many cases, already know and trust. Parents understand that even by the age of five or six, children know when they are driving past a McDonald's. Everybody knows the "Golden Arches" as the McDonald's brand.

- **Support**—As a long-time independent business owner, I can tell you that it gets lonely out there. Without immediate peers or colleagues, you are forced to make many decisions on your own. With franchising, you have a wealth of knowledge waiting there to guide you in your work and, sometimes, just to be there when the going gets rough or it's time to celebrate. You'll also get support from your fellow franchisees. Support from a peer group inside of a franchise is an enormous advantage over an independent operator.

- **Independence**—One of the greatest benefits of franchising is that franchisees get to be part of a team but still work on their own. There is a sense of independence when you're running your own franchise. You can hire your own staff, create your own schedule, and make a lot of decisions independent of the franchisor. Though you might have systems in place you need to follow, you are still in charge of your own enterprise.

- **Risk**—Franchisees might have to give up some control, but they gain the opportunity to share the risk with their franchisor. Though you might make the initial financial investment (and that isn't even true in all cases), the franchisor is as motivated as you to see you succeed. Your franchisor is also invested in your business (since it's also theirs) and will be there to encourage and support your success, as long as you are a partner in those efforts.

- **Training**—From day one, franchisors offer training to help their franchisees properly open and run their businesses. From point of sales to hiring to managing and implementing systems, most franchisees are buying the training as much as the brand. In addition, many franchisors offer ongoing training opportunities so franchisees can benefit from new developments in the industry in which they operate.

- **Financing**—By choosing a franchise, franchisees can often find financing opportunities that might not otherwise be available, whether through a small business loan or through the franchisor themselves. Lenders often take into account the franchisor's experience and reputation when deciding whether or not to lend money. This means that someone might not be able to secure financing on their own but are able to point to the franchise's sales records to support their application. Franchise systems also offer purchasing efficiencies through economies of scale, offering bulk discounts with some or all of the needed products offered by either the franchisor or trusted suppliers.

- **Technical Support**—When problems arise, franchising gives the franchisee an avenue to technical support and qualified staff who can give advice. Most franchises have 800 numbers franchisees can call to get daily support. Other franchises develop peer networks so that they can reach out to one another to ask questions and get feedback as they run and support their businesses.

- **Marketing**—Following the brand and systems is important, but the marketing provided by the franchisor can be crucial to the franchisor's success. From the marketing research performed by the franchise's corporate office to real-time strategies, the franchisor can help franchisees develop better targeting and more effective marketing efforts for franchisees to implement in their communities. In addition, the pooling of resources helps to keep costs reasonable while the shared strategies between franchises support greater brand awareness and cohesion.

- **Transitioning**—If franchisees would like to sell their business at some stage, the franchisor can help locate a new buyer (often for a fee) and assist with the necessary arrangements, as opposed to an independent business owner having to oversee every step of the process alone.

Whether you're looking at McDonald's or a small franchise without the same brand recognition, a franchise offers you a proven system for sales, production, and operations. Once you have a proven, successful concept, it can be repeated over and over again.

Franchising comes from taking what's been created and making it better. From the standpoint of restaurants, how many different franchises are there for submarine sandwiches? A sub sandwich is a sub sandwich. You might like one brand over another, but it's not a new idea. It's just the same concept with a new spin. Even new technology has usually just taken something and evolved it to the next level.

With franchising, you take what was done before, and replicate it in your community. In turn, you get to build a successful business, share the risk of running a business, and build your presence and influence in your community much like they did in the 1500s, because it's true: there are no new ideas.

For more information about franchise opportunities and ideas, visit www.TimsFranchiseBook.com!

Chapter Two:
Is This for Me?

Before we get too far, let me say this: a franchise is not for everyone.

Let's go back to that convention center, the one filled with hundreds of franchise opportunities, and some overwhelmed people, walking in for the first time, wondering what franchising is all about. Every time I meet one of those people, I ask them why they came. *What motivated you?* I ask.

Frequently, I hear that they're tired of corporate life. They want to run their own business. They're looking for more flexibility. They want less work.

And though I never want to be rude, the fact is, they are in the wrong room.

I wish I could say that running a franchise is the perfect escape from corporate life and that you get to go home at 2:00pm and vacation whenever you want. Over time, some—or even most—of those things might come true (including being done at 2:00pm), but while owning a franchise might offer flexibility down the road, opening one demands work, work, work.

When people ask me what they need to become a franchisee, I tell them more than money or connections or ideas, they need one thing: drive.

Lori Greiner from *Shark Tank* says it best: "Entrepreneurs are the only people who will work 80 hours a week to avoid working 40 hours per week."

If you have the necessary drive, working 80 hours a week doesn't feel like work. There are plenty of days I am able to take off and enjoy life, but there are other days I will spend 12 to 16 hours working because I truly enjoy what I do. Knowing that my business is making a difference for the people that franchise with us makes it not feel like work. It feels like fun!

There is a big difference between the dream of owning your own business and the reality, and that difference is a lot of hard work. I tell franchisees to expect to work harder than they ever have in their lives. Still, when you are working for yourself, it doesn't feel the same as when you are working for somebody else. Imagine that you own your own business, whatever you want it to be. Imagine that you are really making a difference in the lives of your team members, their families, your customers, and their families. When you know you are making a difference in so many lives, you can't help but be excited about what you do. As I sit here typing, it is 4:32am, and I'm not even tired because I am so excited about what I am sharing with you.

Beyond that, you also need to know that owning a franchise is not the same as owning your own independent business. With your own business, you write the rules, and you can change the rules; with a franchise, you have to follow someone else's.

Often, I will be talking to someone at one of the shows, and I will ask them if they're good at following directions. It may sound like your third-grade report card, but the truth is, if you've never been good at following instructions—whether those instructions are from your boss, your teachers, or just authority in general—you're going to struggle doing that in a franchise. There is always the temptation to go your own way, but you do so at the risk of losing the business you have put so much time, money, and energy into building.

When you buy a franchise, you are buying a system. It is what makes the business so valuable; if you can't work within the system, you are diminishing the value of your own investment.

Is a Franchise Right for You?

Before we go too far into discussing what kind of franchises are out there, we need to first determine whether franchising is even the right choice for you.

Franchising requires far too much time, effort, and money to realize six years (or even six months) in that it is not a good fit. We'll talk more about finding the right franchise and industry with which you connect, but let's first determine whether the functions of franchising make sense for your interests, goals, and talents.

A few years back, we developed the following quiz to determine whether someone would enjoy being a franchisee. As you take the quiz, remember to answer honestly. I wish I could say that franchising is for everyone, but before you put your hard-earned money and even more hard-earned time into the endeavor, you want to make sure that franchising is right for you.

You can also take our quiz online at www.TimsFranchiseBook.com.

The Compatibility Calculator
Mindsets

	1 2 3	4 5 6	7 8 9	10 11 12	Score	Goal
Ambition	Your past was the best life had to offer. You are in protection mode to preserve what you have.	Your life has been good so far, and you know there is more out there. You don't know where to find it or how to get a piece of it.	Your ambition has allowed you to accomplish a great deal; you are unsure where to turn next.	You see great potential ahead of you. Your best years and most success is still ahead of you. You simply need to go and get it.		
Learning/Growth	You have learned most everything you need to know. There is little for you to learn moving forward.	You have so much to learn, so many areas to grow. You aren't sure others to look for the next place to advance.	You've learned a great deal and value the personal and professional growth from learning, you want to relax in your comfort zone.	You're always interested in learning more. You believe that knowledge will nurture your success.		
Communication	You keep most things to yourself and deal with concerns internally. Likewise, you don't need praise from others, nor offer it to others.	You have difficulty communicating with others even though you know that you need to share information to be more successful.	Your communications skills offer you a sense of control in most situations. You have a good handle on communicating with others.	You communicate with others about most things. You share your concerns and offer positive feedback when it is deserved.		
Personal Responsibility	Your personal success and/or failures are largely a result of external forces of which you have little if any control.	You're trying to take personal responsibility for your actions and decisions, but there are other people that add to the problems.	You take personal responsibility in most circumstances. You know that personal responsibility is a necessary duty.	You're personally responsible for the outcomes of situations in your life be they positive or negative, you own them.		
Take Charge Attitude	You see something that needs attention, but leave it for somebody else to take care of it.	You know and understand the things that need to be done, but there is only so much time to do things and you simply can't do everything.	You take control of most situations but get overwhelmed at times trying to do it all yourself.	You see something that needs to be completed and you simply do it, or delegate it to a responsible party to accomplish the task.		
Risk Tolerance	You see risk as the possibility of losing what you have worked so hard to achieve.	You have taken some risks and they have worked out in your favor. You don't know where to go from here. Dreaming of more is common.	You are satisfied with the success you have achieved through the risks you have taken. Your level of success is comfortable for you.	You see excitement and reward directly associated with risk. The potential reward outweighs the possible risk.		
Commitment	You seek other people's opinions and often change your mind before committing to an option.	You cannot but worry that you have made the wrong decision. You are uneasy if something is unpredictable.	You commit to things easily, but from time to time you question what you are doing and if there is a better way.	You're committed to your ideas. You will not others on your ideas because it takes 100% commitment to achieve growth and success.		
Teamwork	You work independently of others with an attitude of "If I want it done right, I'll have to do it myself."	You know having the right team members in place is a difficult task. You are concerned that a team member could make big mistakes.	You know that teamwork has allowed you to accomplish a great deal. You are comfortable allowing the team to work on their own.	You believe that teamwork is a concept that will lead to greater success when a team works well together with a good leader.		

Courtesy of Image One, 2019.

After you've added up your score, see where you land. The higher your score, the more likely you are to enjoy the benefits and challenges of franchising. After you've had the chance to score yourself, go back and evaluate where you would ultimately like to see yourself.

What areas can you improve upon to strengthen your abilities as a prospective franchisee and a small business owner?

How can you better focus your experience, knowledge, and passion?

How can you improve upon your ability to communicate those skills and commit them to the right endeavor?

How, ultimately, can you learn to better embrace risk and be a part of a team? I have found that you can't have the rewards without the risk, just as you cannot have success without support from others.

Begin to identify your strengths and weaknesses as a business owner, and you will be that much more prepared to run your own business.

It is also important to know your unique abilities. We all have unique aspects of our professional lives that help us achieve success.

A few years back, I was introduced to Dan Sullivan and his Strategic Coach® program. No matter where we are in life, we are always learning. Being a part of entrepreneurial communities has not only helped me to grow and develop as an entrepreneur, but it has also helped me to learn a language around my work.

One of the concepts I have gained from Dan and the Strategic Coach program is that of unique ability, which has been the foundation of his coaching program for entrepreneurs.

As Dan explains, "Your unique ability is the essence of what you love to do and do best. It's your own set of natural talents and the passion that fuels you to contribute in the ways that most motivate you. When articulated, it describes the 'you' that makes you who you are."

We all have a unique ability—that set of natural talents that help us excel in a given industry. For some, it may be technical skills, which could support work as diverse as plumbing or law. For others, it may be their people skills, lending to careers in sales or customer service.

My unique ability has always been my entrepreneurial and leadership skills. When I've been afraid to start a new business or approach a new client, the excitement of a new project always outweighed the fear, propelling me towards success as a business owner. I loved going out and working with clients as much as I loved developing relationships with the people who worked for me, guiding and advising them in their careers.

It is critical that you start by identifying your unique abilities and seeing if and how they would serve you as a franchisee. If you scored well on the quiz or believe you could do the work to get there, the benefits of franchise life can come true, including the ability to vacation when you want and get out of work at 2:00 pm. Imagine having the ability to pick up your kids or go see them at baseball practice after school. Imagine having the opportunity to attend every field trip with your kids and to show up at every game, play, and competition. Imagine having the flexibility to take time off to go on road trips or vacations more than once a year, enjoying the company of your friends and family.

As Joel Weldon, a friend and world-renowned speaking coach, says: "You only have 18 summers with your kids; make them memorable."

My kids are grown. Those 18 summers have long passed, but I am fortunate because owning my own business for all these years allowed me the opportunity to do all those things I told you to imagine.

Now, my boys are grownups. Both are in their 20s and both own and operate Image One franchises; they, too, are benefiting from the entrepreneurial life. They bust their backsides to get things done, they work hard—harder than any of their friends—but they also play hard.

Last year, they both took a month off in June so we could take a family trip: a couple of weeks visiting family and friends followed by 10 days in Alaska. Then in December, they took the month off to spend time with family over the holidays, and we went on our annual ski trip, which I have been doing with them since they were nine and 11 years old. Most young adults don't have the flexibility to take two months off in a single year! If done right, a business can lead to these types of memories for you and your family too.

Remember, as Joel said, you only get 18 summers, but more importantly, you only get one life. Whether you have a family or not, if you are feeling trapped by a 9-to-5 job or know that you are looking for something bigger and more exciting than the work you are doing today, franchising offers you an amazing opportunity to make money and create flexibility while still making you feel like you have people out there who have your back.

If that time is now, don't delay. Don't wait until the time is perfect to start because there is no perfect time. Today is the day.

The question is this: are *you* the person for it?

Franchising is the Halfway Point Between Corporate Life and an Independent Business

So let's say you have just enough money to invest but not enough to build your own business. Or you want independence but are still looking for a safety net. We might have started this chapter talking about all the hard work and rules you need to follow, but franchising is the marriage of the autonomy people seek from an independent business and the systems they appreciate from corporate life.

As I mentioned, there is only a 50% chance that an independent business is going to succeed in its first five years. With a franchise, you have the opportunity to invest in a proven system. Unlike an independent business, you are working with a brand and a business that already has traction and has already proven to be successful within its industry.

Franchises offer entrepreneurs the opportunity to take a proven product that has already been introduced to the market and profit from its success. Some will argue that true entrepreneurs are the ones who start a business from scratch, but as *Forbes* magazine points out, franchisees are entrepreneurs because they take the franchise to a place it hasn't been before[4].

Like Isaac Singer, someone developed the system and/or product, worked out its kinks, and then offered others the chance to duplicate those efforts without the same level of investment. You can never eliminate risk (even the most successful and proven franchises still chance the possibility of failure), but you are able to diminish it.

Still, with that decrease in risk, there is also a decline in control. Everything from the logo to the uniforms to the products you sell have already been chosen for you. You are not only expected to follow these instructions as part of the corporate culture, but you should also be

---

[4] Elgin, Jeff. "Entrepreneurs as Franchisees," *Entrepreneur*, January 2, 2006.

passionate about the culture in which you are invested. It's not to say a vegan can't buy a McDonald's franchise, but why would they?

A franchise offers paint-by-numbers success if you know how to successfully paint by the numbers, but you must also be passionate about the final product. Blindly following orders rarely satisfies people. You must listen to and trust your franchisor.

The more passionate you are about the product and the more you believe in the strategies and systems of the franchisor, the happier and more successful you will likely be.

If you're someone who prefers to do things completely on your own, if you like to think completely out of the box, or if you're someone who doesn't even have a box, you will quickly realize that franchising can be a frustrating endeavor. Those who are always trying to improve the franchise (and that doesn't mean it might not need improving) might find themselves struggling to accept the systems in which they just invested. Not only can that lead them to butt heads with the franchisor, but it can also lend itself to legal conflict if the franchisor is able to prove the franchisee is in violation of the franchise agreement.

Most franchisees sign a 10-year contract with the franchisor; if they're not able to hold up their end of that agreement or struggle with following the requirements of the franchise, they can find themselves going up against companies with much deeper pockets—and a lot more lawyers.

Investing in a franchise is like any other investment. You are choosing to put your money into that specific business because you believe in that business. Unlike a stock, you are putting in untold hours and energy, you are sacrificing time with your family, you are potentially giving up another career or passion altogether. You want to have more than just belief in the company; you need to have a passion for their products, services, and people. You need to care about the value you bring to the franchise, and you need to bring that drive every day in order to meet your goals and the goals of the franchisor.

You may ask yourself: why would I want to invest so much money, time, and energy to be in business for myself? The answer is simple: any time you want something, you have to give up something else. If you want a new car, you have to give up the money to pay for it. If you want to get married, you have to give up the single life. You have to decide what you really want and be willing to give up what it takes to get what you want. When you go into business, as a franchisee or as an independent operator, you have to give up certain things, at least for a period of time. Ultimately, if you're successful, you get more than just a profitable return on your financial investment; you will also receive a return on your time, achieving more freedom to do the things you really enjoy.

In the future, you may be able to sell your business, or it might grow to the point where it runs on "auto-pilot" because you have the right team in place. At that point, you will recognize that the investment you have made was well worth it. You may also ask yourself: is this the right time to go into business for myself? But when is it ever the "right time" to act on a big decision? When is it ever the "right time" to move out of your parents' home? When is it ever the "right time" to get married, or have children, or buy your first home? If you wait until you are 100% ready, you will never act on any of these things. You will never move forward if you keep hanging on to what is comfortable. You can do all the research to find the right franchise or the right business, but if you don't act, you can't move forward with your goal of being a business owner. A goal without action is just a dream.

Working in janitorial services, I frequently competed with unit-franchisees of the big national franchise companies. I would meet the owners and wonder why they just didn't go out on their own, but as I started working in franchising, I realized that not everyone has had the same experiences I did. I grew up in a family where owning and running your own business was second nature, but not many people were running their own independent business by the time they were 14.

As I said, one of my unique abilities has always been entrepreneurship; I love developing systems for companies. I love building from the ground up, though trust me, I made a million mistakes getting there. Over the years, I have realized that isn't everyone's passion. For some, the task of starting a business is simply too overwhelming; the moment they make their first big mistakes—and experience the associated consequences—they want out.

Of course, there were times when I wanted out too, but I had a drive for independent businesses. Once I got into franchising, I realized the opportunity they offered: the chance for people to get into business for themselves with an already established system. Someone else had made the million mistakes and paid the steep consequences so I didn't have to. A key tagline for all franchise systems is: "Be in business for yourself, but not by yourself." That statement holds a great deal of value. A franchise really does allow you all the benefits of being in business for yourself, but if you pick the right franchise, you will have an incredible support system to help you nearly every step of the way.

As I said, I have never been in a job interview, and I have never been a part of corporate life. In fact, the only job I have ever had as someone else's employee was when I was 16 and I worked at the corner gas station/car wash with two of my buddies. The funny thing is my office cleaning business was already successful, so I was making six times less at the car wash for minimum wage ($3.25 at the time). As you may have guessed, I wasn't doing it for the money. It was just about having fun with my friends. There was no manager on duty for much of the time, so the three of us got to run the show and got paid doing it.

Though I never really had a "real" job working for somebody else, I do understand why the stability of corporate life can be attractive. You have health benefits and 14 days of paid vacation; for the most part, there is little risk. But you also never get the rewards of a self-employed individual.

Oftentimes, people look at business owners and think they have it easy. They have the nice car and nice house, they travel, and it seems like it all came pretty easily. Fact is, we didn't see the business owner go through the rough times. My business wasn't an overnight success unless you consider 30 years to be overnight. Once I got into franchising, I wondered whether it might have been easier had I joined my competitors and become a franchisee years ago. But through my mistakes, I have developed a system with Image One that I can now share with others. I have paid the price so others don't have to.

If my franchisees are willing to work hard, follow the system, and be passionate about their work, they're able to achieve success, achieve flexibility, and yes, on some days, leave at 2:00pm to catch their kid's afternoon game.

To learn more about finding the right franchise for you, visit www.TimsFranchiseBook.com!

Chapter Three:
Franchising - It's Not Just
Frozen Yogurt

Back in the late 1980s, it felt like you couldn't go a block without seeing a TCBY Yogurt. They were everywhere, and it appeared everyone was buying that franchise. For a lot of people, when you mention a franchise, that's what they think about: TCBY. Or McDonald's. Most people don't realize just how many types of franchises exist.

Franchising goes way beyond frozen yogurt and hamburgers.

If you are looking to start a new franchise business, it's important to know which industry you would like to be involved in, the level of financial commitment you have available or can raise, and how much of a time commitment will be involved.

What most people are surprised to discover is that just about every type of business has been franchised. From single owner operator, to home-based, to brick-and-mortar, there are countless models of franchises. There are business to consumer (B2C) and business-to-business (B2B) opportunities. There are investment-based franchises, master franchises, and area developers. You can even buy a franchise that assists people in buying their own franchise!

The *unit model* is the most well-known model of franchising; this is where the franchisor will usually expect only a percentage return from its franchisees but will retain control over product development, branding, and distribution.

My introduction to franchises came through a master franchise. A *master franchisee* is a sub-franchise granted by a franchisor to someone who will then sell unit-franchises, usually in a specific state, region, or internationally. A unit-franchisee is buying the company from the master franchiser, which acts as the middle man between the unit and the larger franchisor. Not all industries have master franchises, but it's fairly commonplace in the janitorial industry.

For the sake of this book, I am going to limit my discussion to unit franchises where the franchisee is dealing directly with the franchisor.

Everyone has a different reason for wanting to acquire a franchise. Some want to make an investment and others want to be hands-on. Some might want to sell multi-unit franchises—perhaps a group of franchise locations, maybe two or three, or maybe even 35 restaurants. In that case, your job would just be to oversee the management of those units. Other people might only be interested in a single-unit franchise where they go in and work every day. Finding the right franchise depends on how much time, effort, energy, and money you're looking to invest.

Different Types of Franchises

Most people don't realize how many different types of franchises exist. In fact, a lot of people don't recognize that many of the businesses they visit as consumers are franchises—from plumbers to restaurants to dry cleaning to the little kiosks at the mall that sell cell phone covers.

Franchises are split up by multiple business sectors, interests, and industries (which we will discuss in further detail later), but can also be organized into four distinct franchise structures based on the ways in which they operate and the level of investment required for participation. These types include:

1. **Service Franchises**—These franchises typically involve a single operator selling products or providing a service within a specific trade or industry. In this type of franchise, the franchisor provides the brand name or trademark together with relevant equipment, uniforms, and marketing material in order for the franchisee to sell the products or deliver the services to an established standard and reputation. With smaller levels of investment, this type of franchise is suitable for home-based businesses, mobile operators, or smaller start-up businesses. Often, these types of franchises will include accountants,

products, or skill trainers and consultants interested in utilizing the brand's recognition and quality in order to expand their business.

A wide and diverse range of services—including travel agencies, coffee vans, domestic lawn care services, plumbing, drain cleaning, commercial and domestic cleaning, cell phone accessories and repairs, real estate services, shipping services, pool maintenance, corporate event planning, and children's services—fall into this group.

Most of these businesses go directly to their customer, which greatly reduces their capital expenditure. Janitorial services fall into this category. Our franchisees do not rent retail space and are able to own and operate the business from home because the work is being done at the clients' facility. IT franchises work in the same way, providing the service at their customer's location rather than their own.

2. **Product Franchises**—These franchises are based on supplier-dealer relationships where the franchisee distributes the franchisor's products. The franchisor licenses its trademark but may not provide franchisees an entire system for running their business.

Product franchises deal mainly with large products such as cars, car parts, motorcycles and other recreational vehicles, vending machines, computers, bicycles, or appliances. Product distribution franchising represents the highest percentage of total retail sales.

Some well-known product distribution franchises are Exxon, Texaco, Goodyear Tires, John Deere, Ford, Chrysler, and other automobile producers. Sometimes franchisor licenses are not only for distribution but also for part of the manufacturing process, such as soft drink manufacturers Coca-Cola and Pepsi.

The franchisor offers a detailed plan and procedures on almost every aspect of the business and provides initial and ongoing training and support. Product franchising is the most popular type of franchise system. Businesses from more than 70 industries can be franchised, the most popular being fast food, retail, restaurant, and fitness.

This type of franchise will usually be owner-operated from a retail outlet and will serve walk-in customers. These tend to require the right location and customer base. Because many of these franchises are brick-and-mortar, they can require a significant investment, which includes rent and construction costs for the retail unit. An example of a franchise of this type—which is currently experiencing a boom—are child-based facilities like child care centers, children's gyms, and pools built specifically for children's swim lessons.

Franchisees may buy old office buildings and dig out an Olympic-size pool under them to create a swim center. There is obviously a massive expense in that. No one quits their five-figure job to open up a swimming pool.

On the other hand, maybe the location is one of those kiosks at the mall where they sell cell phone covers and chargers. Maybe the capital investment is simply the cost of renting a cart, which can be a lot more realistic for most first-time franchisees.

Whether it's retail, restaurants, or any number of products and services in between, the level of investment determines just how big your brick-and-mortar operation can be. Once you get into the work, your ability to manage the pieces of that investment will determine your success.

3. **Investment Franchises**—Typically, these are grand-scale projects that require a significant capital investment, such as hotels, department stores, and larger restaurants. The franchisees

usually invest money and hire a management team to operate the business, which will produce an ROI and capital gain on exit. The franchisee will normally work in a managerial and advisory role, overseeing a large team of employees. The franchisee, often a corporate investor, will delegate the running of the business to an executive team.

4. **Conversions & Master Franchising**—Many franchise systems grow by converting independent businesses in the same industry into franchise units. The franchisees adopt trademarks, marketing and advertising programs, training systems, and critical client service standards. This type of franchise is typically run from regional or geographic head offices and involves the development, management, and coordination of a group of operatives or team of providers for the service or product. Master franchises can grow rapidly in terms of units and royalty fee income. Some examples of industries that use master franchising are real-estate brokers, florists, professional services companies, and home services like plumbing, electricians, and air conditioning.

What kind of business do you want to run?

We've talked a great deal about the different opportunities that exist in franchising, and perhaps you are feeling as overwhelmed as the person who walks into the convention center for the first time and sees all the options that are available. How do you narrow down the field of opportunities? It shouldn't be a surprise that the first and perhaps most-important factor here is money.

You can have all the passion and time and energy in the world, but if the McDonald's franchise you want to buy costs $1 million, and you only have $20,000, the Golden Arches are probably not going to be in your immediate future.

Let's head back to that franchise show.

You walk in and make it past the front atrium. Now you're walking down the rows, and you see something that piques your interest. Let's say it's CrossFit, which is all the rage these days among fitness franchises.

Imagine that as the prospective franchisee, you love CrossFit, and you've identified a need for one in your own neighborhood. Let's say the franchisor was already running market research in your community. As a probable franchisee, you also have the money. The nice thing about CrossFit is that the equipment, though substantial, still costs less than a traditional gym.

You talk to a CrossFit franchisor and they decide to move the conversation forward.

Meanwhile, in another aisle, an IT analyst walks the tech row. He's currently working for an accounting firm and is considering going freelance, but doesn't want the risk of starting out on his own. Our franchisee doesn't have a lot of money to invest but has experience and know-how. He meets an IT franchisor who connects IT specialists with companies and individuals in need of on-call help. It will allow the franchisee to work from home and design his own schedule, with the support of an established name and company.

In both cases, the prospective franchisee has been able to connect with a franchisor that fits. You with CrossFit, and the IT guy with the tech firm. The IT guy will likely have no interest in CrossFit, and you will similarly have no interest in technology. There is a fit for each of you in the industry that you find interesting.

I cannot emphasize enough how important that fit is. As you will hear me say many times throughout the course of this book, franchising is like marriage. If you don't connect with your franchisor from the start, it's unlikely to get better over time. You need to be on the same page from day one.

So, how do you narrow the field of available franchise opportunities? Start by asking yourself these questions:

- Do you have the funds to invest?

- How much time are you looking to invest?

- Do you want to be involved in the daily working of the business?

- Do you have the skills and background for the type of franchising you are considering?

We will discuss doing due diligence on the franchise in greater detail later; first, you need to perform some due diligence on yourself. Just as you are investing in the franchise, the franchise is investing in you. You want to make sure that you are both achieving a satisfactory ROI. Based on your potential investment of skills, time, money, and expertise in franchising, what is the right fit for you?

Money is just the first part of finding your fit. While you don't have to have a passion or interest in the work you're doing, you need to have an understanding of why it's important. I always say that I didn't grow up thinking, "I want to scrub toilets for a living," but I did grow up wanting to run a business that would have me interacting with people every day, that would provide a stable income, and that would provide me with the opportunity for personal and professional growth.

By looking at cleaning from a different point of view, our franchisees realize that, ultimately, it is about the safety of thousands of people every day. Ensuring people's health is something people can get passionate about!

Later, when I was no longer the guy actually scrubbing the toilets, I realized that it was also my passion for running a successful business that made us so successful. You don't always have to love the labor, but you do need to love the service it provides your customers.

Naturally, finances are a huge thing, but once you figure out how much of a franchise you can afford, the next question is: what kind of franchise do you want to run?

26%	25%	23%	20%	6%
Food	Services	Retail	Home-Based	Other

Courtesy of Franchise Direct, 2017.

Are you interested in selling a service or a product? Is this something you want to run out of your own home, or would you need retail and/or office space? Do you want to stay in your current location, or would you be open to traveling or even relocating for the franchise?

Depending on the franchise you are looking at, you may have to relocate to an area they have available. Some years ago, a good friend of mine wanted to open a Harley Davidson® dealer. He had been riding motorcycles his entire life and had experience owning a couple of different businesses over the years. He was a great fit for the franchise.

Unfortunately, there were no franchise opportunities available where he lived, and the timing wasn't right for him to pick up and move several states away to an available territory.

Another consideration: are you interested in working with customers directly, or would you prefer to be with a business-to-business industry? If you are working with consumers, do you want to see your customer? Getting to know our customers is one of the great joys of my work. But an IT tech, for example, might prefer to work remotely, focused on a computer, offering his service in a 15-minute call without any further customer engagement.

Another question is: what is your background? Virtually anyone could open a kiosk in the mall selling cell phone covers. You don't need to have a degree for that. But not everyone could buy into a plumbing and mechanical franchise. Having a background in the trades would surely be beneficial for such a business. Where does your experience, education, and trade intersect with the franchise industry?

Finally, ask yourself: is there something I really love that I would love to see realized through a franchise? Maybe you love animals and are interested in pet grooming or walking services. Maybe you want to open up a doggy daycare. If you are a teacher and love working with kids, an after school tutoring program might be the answer.

Maybe your franchise isn't about the service you offer in your community, but about an interest you have longed to pursue—like yoga or nutrition or running a restaurant.

How do your experiences, abilities, and passions converge? Can these three domains converge in one franchise? This isn't always the case. Sometimes we have to sacrifice one element for the rest (or are limited by one element over the others), but the closer we can get to the bullseye of our abilities and interests, the more likely we are to succeed.

Ask for Help

If you're struggling to figure out what franchise is right for you, some people find working with a franchise broker or consultant helps them find the best fit. (Check out TimsFranchiseBook.com for a list of potential brokers and consultants.) There are many brokers and consultants who work in the franchise industry to assist you; some are franchisees themselves. (While the term broker and consultant are not 100% interchangeable, we will call them all brokers for simplicity.) The process is quite simple. First, the broker needs to get to know you. The broker will likely spend time asking you questions about your back-ground, your interests, and your financial status. Getting to know you is key to that person helping you find what is right for you; you should have to complete a questionnaire and talk about your goals, work history, and the desired timing of your new endeavor.

The right broker will narrow down the field of opportunities for you and could save you a great deal of time and frustration. Brokers can't do all the work for you, but they will offer you different franchise opportunities that seem to be a good fit. It is then up to you to review the opportunities and conduct your due diligence on each of them throughout the process.

Most people think that if the brokers are doing all of this work, they must be expensive to use. The good news is, it doesn't cost you a penny. The broker gets paid by the franchisor for finding you. There is no cost or obligation to you, and many franchisors like the idea of using brokers because they know the people recommended are pre-qualified, motivated, and often-times better informed than other potential franchisees. It is similar to a real estate transaction: the realtor may be working to find you a home but is ultimately paid by the seller in the transaction. The broker can help guide you to a good fit. Knowing what you want when you speak to a franchisor will make the process much easier.

At Image One, we know that most people are like me; they don't come to janitorial services with a passion for scrubbing toilets. Most come with the passion for being in business for themselves, as well as for helping people, and that passion intersects with the financial stability commercial cleaning provides.

As a franchise owner of any business, your daily routine shouldn't be scrubbing toilets for hours each day, or making sub-sandwiches all day long, or being the fry-guy. If that's what you love, do it, but the most successful franchisees in any business model spend their time working ON their business, not IN their business. In other words, you want to work on building a solid business that will operate with or without you. Don't get hung up on the product or service that the franchise offers. You don't want to overlook a concept simply because it isn't a sexy business. Most of those businesses are the ones that turn out to be a fad or are short lived. Whether or not you decide to use a broker, find a franchise that is a good fit—something you can see yourself doing for a long period of time.

As I said, franchises are like marriages. You are not only getting involved in a long-term commitment, you're making a legal commitment to one another as well. While a marriage is a lot more personal, a franchise can be pretty personal, too.

The franchise agreement that you will sign is one (as we will soon learn) that might even hold you to certain profit goals. If the going gets tough, you can't always just walk away. Your decision is going to be a long-term commitment, so it needs to be with the right franchise. A divorce is generally a messy, expensive, unpleasant experience most people would like to avoid. Getting out of a business agreement can be equally uncomfortable (and can cost even more).

As you narrow down the field to determine which franchise is right for you, you need to identify which structure is the best fit for your interests and capabilities.

Though life in independent business can be risky and life in a corporate environment can get dull, "The grass is greener where you water it."

Franchising takes an enormous amount of tending. You have to be out there every day with your hose, nurturing it and putting out fires. Then you have to be able to pay for the water you just used.

It has to be something that fits with your wallet but also something you really enjoy. If you don't enjoy it, why do it?

I hope by now you have figured out if being a franchisee is a good fit. If you haven't figured it out just yet, that's okay too. Choosing a business is a major decision. Don't hesitate to call a broker and see if he or she can help you find the right fit. I promise, if franchising is a good fit for your unique ability and the vision you have for your life, it's only a matter of time and research before you find the right fit. Be patient, do the work, and you will find the business to help you achieve all your personal and professional goals.

If you need more help making your choice, check out www.TimsFranchiseBook.com for more support.

Chapter Four:
Picking Your Passion
(When Possible)

We don't always get to do what we're passionate about in life, but it sure is nice when we do. That said, I always tell people there is a difference between *doing* something you love and *buying* something you love. You might love frozen yogurt, but that doesn't mean you should own a TCBY. The most important thing is: can you be as passionate about selling your product as you feel about buying your product?

Though a key part of finding the right franchise is determining the right business structure for your financial and professional capabilities, the other prerequisite is determining what type of business you would be interested in running.

For those interested in food, the options go beyond owning a restaurant. You can work with an organic food company or a cooking franchise, among many other food-related businesses.

Likewise, if you're interested in working with children, you could invest in a childcare franchise or a tutoring agency. You could buy a coding company that teaches kids how to code, or a chess club agency which helps them win chess competitions.

You don't have to work within your field of interest, but most people find it easier to run a business they understand.

Like I said, that's not to say that your dream in life has to be cleaning services, but if you absolutely hate cleaning, a janitorial or housekeeping franchise probably isn't for you.

I've actually always enjoyed cleaning. Even when I was the one doing the tough labor, there was a peace in the work that motivated me to develop the best systems for my business. Even now, when I go out and strip and refinish a floor with a new franchisee, there is a sense of pride and accomplishment. I still love finishing a job, and saying, "I did that!" If I didn't love what I did, I wouldn't have worked to perfect it. Through my passion for service, I was determined to run the best janitorial service in town.

When I became a franchisor, I was able to pass down systems I spent years perfecting because I loved my job and cared about what I did. Even more than that, we have worked hard to create a system that works for our franchisees' progress and success. We have invested hundreds of thousands of dollars in technology and software to help them acquire and maintain clients. We have introduced iPad® apps and software that nobody else in our industry even dreams about. When our franchisees meet with prospective clients, they are amazed at how technologically advanced Image

One is compared to our competitors, many of whom still write out estimates on a legal pad.

Launching a unit franchise is a massive investment of money, time, and energy, so it makes sense to love the work—or at least be passionate about its outcomes for your clients and the community. If you are able to find a franchise you care about and whose mission you understand, you'll be halfway to running a successful business.

Top Franchise Industries

Over the last 20 years, some new industries have popped up that now dominate the franchise field— namely, child-oriented and health-oriented franchises— yet, some things remain the same (like the popularity of quick-service restaurants). As I said earlier, there are no new ideas; even the new industries found their foundation in other existing businesses. "New ideas" are just new methods of delivery, or advancements on existing products or services.

While some industries might not be a possibility for you based on your financial resources and other necessary investments, if you have more flexibility, you can look at what interests and passions you would like to pursue. Once you know the type of franchise you want to pursue, you can find the one that fits.

Every year, *Entrepreneur* magazine puts out the top 50 franchise industries. The top 10 have remained relatively the same over the last decade (although there is usually one surprise on the list). Let's take a look at the top five from 2018.

Quick-service restaurants

Quick-service restaurants comprise more than 20% of all franchise industries, making it the biggest sector of the industry by far. Over the last few years, however, there have been shifts within the industry. Though fast-food companies still dominate, three specific franchise trends have entered the field: fast and casual eateries, healthier foods, and international cuisines. Companies that have been franchising for decades have high speed and low prices locked up, so newcomers look to compete on food quality and atmosphere.

Fast and casual restaurants have ballooned in response to people's criticism of the big fast food chains; they offer a more intimate dining experience with the convenience of a fast food franchise. Some of these include Five Guys, Chipotle Mexican Grill, Shake Shack, Boston Market, Bruegger's, Panera Bread, Smashburger, and Zaxby's.

As more and more people continue to adopt healthier lifestyles and greater food consciousness, healthier quick-service options have sprung up across the country, like vegetarian restaurant Veggie Grill, Freshii with its green wraps and quinoa bowls, and Sweetgreen, a fast and casual restaurant focused on salads.

Another growing restaurant trend is the demand for international cuisines, such as Asian-inspired foods. The poké craze continues, and more and more companies are looking to capitalize on it through franchising. Other international menus continue to thrive as well. From noodle shops to taco shacks, new franchise options appear all the time.

Beauty Services

People are also still committed to beauty and grooming services, with a new explosion in dry bars, eyelash and hair extensions, and massage services. Pampering yourself is in, and it doesn't look like it's going anywhere. Nail care salons have led this industry for some time and still carry the share of the market, but as those businesses add more services, more specialized businesses have entered. That's why personal-care businesses like waxing and spray-tan salons are embracing the franchise model.

This trend doesn't just apply to women; there are a number of brands that cater to image-conscious men. From barber shops to shaving parlors, businesses have been hopping on the trend for retro-styled grooming services for men. Pretty soon, you will be seeing barber quartets singing outside your local franchise (if you haven't already)!

Children's businesses

Kids are big business, thanks to all the parents who are willing to invest in them. With more and more parents working, the demand for childcare is high, so it's no surprise that childcare franchises have experienced impressive growth in recent years. In this industry, well-known brands continue to dominate, especially those that also provide educational services.

From companies that offer preschoolers a head start to tutoring services that help high-schoolers boost SAT scores, franchises are earning high marks by supplementing the traditional education system. In addition, as US students continue to fall behind in the hard sciences, there has been a surge in educational franchises involving STEM (science, technology, engineering and mathematics). Tutoring franchise Mathnasium has flourished as have other math- and science-based franchises.

For many people who have a background in education or childcare, children's businesses can be a great—and lucrative—way to apply their skillsets without the bureaucracy of working for a school district or the inflexibility of working as a personal childcare provider. Franchising is an ideal way for people experienced in working with children to make money and have more free time in their schedule.

Fitness

Fitness is one of the biggest franchise industries—and one that continues to grow year after year. There's something for everyone—including kids, who have a large number of sports and fitness franchises aimed at them.

Where big-box gyms were once the norm, fitness studios with smaller footprints and specialized workouts are succeeding by creating a more personal experience for clients and keeping costs down for franchisees. More than one-third of the ranked fitness franchises can be started for less than $100,000.

Whether you're interested in a major gym, a barre class, a gymnasium for kids, or CrossFit (like our previous example), you should be able to find a range of franchises in the fitness industry. Not everyone has the funds to open a Gold's Gym, but many can jump on board with a smaller yoga or fitness studio.

Maintenance

I'm sure you're not surprised to see maintenance on this list. With their super-low startup costs, commercial cleaning franchises have long been among the most popular choices for aspiring business owners on a budget. Also increasingly popular are environmentally-friendly solutions to maintenance problems that might ordinarily require chemicals, like interior and exterior cleaning, pest control, and odor elimination.

As I have discovered as a maintenance franchisor, commercial and residential cleaning services are great for first-time franchisees, as they offer a significant return without a substantial investment, opening the door to many franchisees who might not otherwise be able to run and operate their own business.

Of course, there are hundreds more options out there to fit your interests, skills, and passions. As the following flow chart humorously shows, there are plenty of options out there depending on what you like to do—and how "bendy" you happen to be.

Courtesy of Franchise Direct, 2012.

Though the above chart is done partially in jest, it doesn't hurt to ask yourself similar questions:

- What industries have you always been interested in—not just as a consumer but as a potential business owner?

- What are your hobbies and passions?

- Where do your personal interests intersect with your personal experiences?

- What franchises align with that intersection?

- What industries are both financially viable and personally interesting to you?

- How can you connect with one today?

As I have said, the most important aspect of finding the right franchise is discovering the right fit, not just in terms of finance and investment, but also your interests and passions.

You would probably be surprised to find that even in the more capital-heavy franchises, there are less-expensive options. As in food service, there are small cafés, ice cream shops, and dessert and specialty foods that wouldn't demand the same footprint or investment as a McDonald's.

Once you know what type of franchise you are interested in and what kind of business structure fits your means, you can begin doing the real research to find the one that fits.

First, you need to take a step back and determine what kind of franchise you qualify for rather than what kind of franchise qualifies for you.

Chapter Five:
Starting with the Upfront

According to the International Franchise Association, franchise businesses are growing at a faster rate than non-franchises. For the past five years, the average annual job growth in the franchise sector was 2.6%, nearly 20% higher than other businesses.

Naturally, the franchise world is thrilled about this progress. For a lot of people, franchises are an attractive way to own a business with the safety net of an established brand and systems.

In recent years, the economic track record for franchises has been strong as well, with growth across most sectors of the industry. Because franchises are themselves an investment, most people want to know what their rate of return is going to be. As we've discussed, however, that ROI depends as much on you as on the franchisor.

Being a franchisee demands a big investment, not just of money, but of time, attention, and energy as well.

There are risks to every investment, but in the case of franchises, the biggest risk is often you.

That can be a tough pill to swallow. At the end of the day, if the ROI isn't there, you won't have a company or a board to blame; you will only have yourself.

This is why when determining what kind of franchise you want to invest in, you need to decide not just where you're going to get your best ROI but where you're going to get your best Return on You (ROY).

Though a lot of people will talk about financial yield, I would say the return on your time, talents, and abilities is just as (if not more) important. Your ROY won't just put money in your bank account; it's the difference between living a fulfilled or frustrated life. You don't want to feel like you are getting back way less than you are putting in. You want to go home every day tired but knowing that the hard work you put in was worth it.

The main reason people leave W2 employment isn't the ROI. It's that they're not getting the return on themselves that they feel is fair and in line with their talents and abilities.

You are choosing your franchise. Make sure it's one that is going to give you so much ROI, you'll have no choice but to feel fulfilled.

Investment of Money

But Tim, I thought we already went over this!

We did, but the finances are *that* important. We need to go over it again.

For a lot of people, a franchise can look like a great way to buy a business. This is why, after the 2008 Global Financial Crisis, there was an uptick in franchise operations. As the non-franchise employment market shrunk, folks started looking for other employment opportunities. Some were interested in transitioning out of W2 life, looking for more flexibility and purpose. For others, the choice didn't come from them, but rather from a changing marketplace in which a number of large industries were threatened by the global financial crisis. Either way, a number of new prospects saw franchises as a great investment. That said, those investments can be costly.

The cost of the franchise depends on the type and size of the business; no matter what it is, it will require an upfront investment, starting with the franchise fee. Franchise fees vary greatly. Some range from $15,000 to $50,000, but they can go as high as $100,000 or more. In some cases, this includes the cost of training; in others, you have to pay for portions of the training. In the United States, the franchise fee for Subway is $15,000, but the total investment to open a Subway restaurant is estimated to be between $116,000 and $263,000.

Still, there are many franchises that can be launched for less than $60,000, with many at-home service franchises starting from $4,000 to $15,000.

As we've discussed, the type of franchise you're buying determines the price. It also determines what else you'll need in order to open the business—from equipment to retail space to uniforms to transportation. Based on the level of investment, and the anticipated initial revenue, ROI can vary widely across different franchise industries. In most cases, the return (expressed as a percentage of the total investment) is usually smaller on high-investment franchise opportunities than on low-investments opportunities.

We'll talk about the Franchise Disclosure Document (FDD) in greater detail later, but when you decide on your franchise, all the financials will be articulated in the FDD, including any additional fees, payments, or royalties owed to the franchisor. Most franchisors expect an ongoing royalty. The range of royalty varies greatly, from as low as 1% to as high as 50%. An average royalty will be from 5-6%; you need to factor that in when estimating your profits.

In addition, you might need to pay into the franchisor's advertising and marketing budgets since franchisees ultimately benefit from the franchisor's marketing efforts—whether they're national, regional, or local. You might have to attend national conferences or trainings and cover the travel costs for you and even your staff. There might be other fees or costs from the franchisor, but they should all be agreed upon prior to signing the franchise agreement (the legal contract which binds the franchisee to the franchisor).

The good thing about the franchise industry is that it's regulated, which means there are no surprise fees or payments. You only pay for what's outlined in the FDD, so as you consider different franchises, you are able to anticipate your initial investment and yield.

Early in the process, the franchisor will provide the franchisee with their FDD, a legal document required by the Federal Trade Commission (FTC). The FDD offers a wealth of information, including an audited financial statement of the franchisor's earnings. Item 19 of the FDD is dedicated to Financial Performance Representations. Though not required by the FTC, many FDD's include an Item 19, which offers an overview of the financial performance of existing franchised units and how a particular franchise might perform in the future. It does not, however, discuss the actual performance of an existing business.

Franchisors have complete freedom to select the type of Item 19 disclosure that makes sense for their businesses. For hotel systems, this may include occupancy rates; restaurants may include gross sales figures; car washes might include daily car counts and average ticket numbers. Some franchisors show complete profit and loss statements; others show simple presentations of average gross sales figures.

While an Item 19 disclosure may be industry-specific, the more an investor knows about the franchise system's financial performance, the better. With more information in hand, you are in a far better position to do your own financial planning.

Of course, things will always come up—especially if you're opening a new space or have a large capital budget—but those franchises with fewer moving parts—such as tech, janitorial, or other low-capital services—

allow business owners to more accurately estimate expenses.

Next, you need to secure your funding. Some franchisees might already have the money in the bank for start-up costs. Franchises will occasionally help with the financing, connecting prospective franchisees with loans and lending opportunities.

While you might have to go out and get it yourself, there are a number of great small business loans to help you to get your franchise off the ground.

We will discuss financing in greater detail later, but as you begin to consider the size and scale of different franchises, know that your investment can be much larger than the cash you currently have on hand.

You can also leverage other assets, such as real estate investments, your 401k, and other investment products or trusts. And of course, there are always your friends and family members who might be willing to make an investment if you are confident in the return. The thing to remember is that there is always a risk, but with the right franchise, it can be a risk well worth taking.

This is why you want to be able to estimate what your first three years in business will look like. You can reach out to the franchisor and other franchisees to determine the average earnings of a typical unit during their first three years of operation. If a business is not making their returns by the third year, you might be better off if you keep shopping. There are plenty of other opportunities that will earn out in the same or less time.

Just as you need to think about your own strengths, weaknesses, costs and potential earnings of a franchise, you also need to consider present and future economic trends. We are moving from a manufacturing to a tech economy, and franchises are making a similar transition. There are very few sewing machine franchises anymore, but every day a new tech-related franchise is launched. Review the recent track record of success for the potential franchise opportunity you are considering— the number of openings, closings, transfers, and terminations—but also consider their products and services in relation to the economy and where the economy is headed.

In addition, where you live (and ultimately want to run your franchise), can greatly affect the franchise you want to run. Some franchises aren't available nationally, and likewise, some perform better in some regions than others.

Make sure to investigate how well a specific franchise has succeeded in your state, region, and even neighborhood. Some franchises do better in specific communities than others, and though most franchisors will have this market data, there is no reason to pursue a franchise that is doomed to fail in the wrong neighborhood.

Finding the right franchise is all about finding the one that works for you—and one that will continue to work five, 10, even 15 years down the road.

Investment of Energy

The difference between investing in a franchise and investing in the stock market is simple: both require money, but only one requires your time. Franchising is not a passive investment. In addition to your capital and time, you're also investing your talent, which means you want a return on more than just your financial investment. That's why I say it's not just ROI, it's ROY too.

Usually, like most investments, the capital you put in will be static. As a result, you can look at what you intend to put in for the franchise fee, royalties, equipment, staff, uniforms, and all the other expenses, and compare that to what you anticipate to see in profit. That won't be your real return though because you've left out one major piece of the investment—you.

You are your greatest asset. For less money than what it would cost to open your own business, you can leverage your time and talent. A strong franchise system should be able to help you transform those assets into a timely and profitable return. Your gross revenue will vary from franchise to franchise, and your profit margin will vary greatly as well, which means your personal income will be determined as much by external factors as by internal ones. If you open a restaurant in downtown Chicago, you will pay much higher rent than if you open in a suburban strip mall. Similarly, if you open in a city or state that has a higher minimum wage, or a higher cost of living, you will have to charge a higher fee for your products or services to cover your cost of labor.

People who don't have a lot of financial capital, or who are partnering with investors to make up for that lack, need to consider how much sweat equity the franchise will demand. If you're going to be working 80 hours a week, you're going to want to see a sizable return on that time. Otherwise, you will only be frustrated by your investment yet still legally obligated to your franchisor.

Remember, if you are working 80 hours a week, the work you are doing is only worth the wage you would pay somebody else to do the same. You can't expect to earn $100,000 per year if you are simply the sandwich maker or the fry guy. The return isn't just based on the number of hours you invest, but the level of compensation those hours would beget. In order to achieve your goals, you want your profit to do more than just match your compensation.

Successful franchisees are able to set realistic expectations, accurately determine their inputs, and be happy with the anticipated outcomes. If you give your all to a business that doesn't provide in return, neither you nor your franchisor will be pleased with the investment, and most importantly, you won't be fulfilled by your work. I promise you, all the profit in the world doesn't buy fulfillment. That can only come when you are getting an ROY that honors your time, talents, and yourself.

Investment of Time

You can always get your money back, but you can never reclaim your time. Whenever I see a really bad movie, I always say, "Well, that's two hours I'll never get back!"

Working your franchise can feel the same way. You will not get back the time you invest unless that investment leads to a return of your time later. Investing 60 or even 80 hours a week when your business is brand new can allow you the time to enjoy yourself when your business is mature. Remember, my kids took two full months off last year! When they started their franchise, they would manage the sales and marketing during the day, and, on most nights, would be swinging a mop well after midnight until they had enough of a crew trained to complete the daily cleaning without them.

But you shouldn't only account for the time you put into working on and in the business. You need to also consider the time you will spend waiting for the business to grow.

The franchise won't open the day after you sign the franchise agreement. In fact, if you're opening a new location, it might take months to even a year or more to determine the location, negotiate the lease, design the space, line up the necessary permits, begin construction, and open the store.

Service-based industries might take less time, but even then the staff might need to be hired and trained, and it might be a while before business starts rolling in.

In any circumstance, franchisees must be financially prepared to work a lot of hours with little-to-no pay at the business' start (and usually at some level of expense). They must be prepared for that time-line to go longer than expected.

Often, franchisees will get frustrated during this period. Unfortunately, the franchisee's timetable doesn't always align with that of the franchisor. The franchisee might be ready to open tomorrow but the franchisor isn't in as big of a rush. They already have an established income. In situations where the franchisee might need to wait for the franchisor to give approval or even feedback, the franchisee can find themselves waiting longer than anticipated.

It can be a hard first lesson of franchising that the franchisee is not a stand-alone company. Franchise owners cannot make decisions, or at least not as quickly as they might on their own. They are part of a larger brand and being part of that brand means they need to work within the system.

Again, finding the right franchise isn't just about your abilities and capabilities; it's also about the franchise in which you invest. As part of your due diligence, you need to ask some hard questions around timeline:

- How quickly does the franchise usually take to respond to franchisees?

- How long did it take for other franchises to open and start performing?

- What are the anticipated hurdles to opening this specific franchise?

- How does the franchise support franchisees in these processes?

- What are some of the workarounds offered by the franchise when confronted with project delays?

All FDDs include a list of current and former franchise partners. Be sure to call some of them. Ask them some of the questions above. The franchisor may suggest that you call some specific franchisees, and that is okay, but also call a few they don't suggest. If they had difficulties, or things didn't go exactly as they expected, they will share that information with you. Don't be discouraged if you hear some negative things. It won't all be 100% positive; it simply can't be. This is the best way to determine how the franchise works, its biggest challenges, and how it has supported (or failed to support) franchisees in the process.

You need to ask yourself similarly hard questions as well. You need to do your due diligence on your own financial capabilities and ask:

- How long are you able to go without direct income?

- Will you be able to sustain your life and lifestyle even beyond the anticipated timeline?

- What are the anticipated hurdles (personally and/or professionally) you might need to overcome in order to open the franchise?

- How will you manage such challenges?

Though the financials are key, you need to ensure that your time, energy, and talents are also seeing a return. You are offering the franchise much more than money; you are offering them yourself.

You Need to Do More than Build It

Unlike in the movie *Field of Dreams*, you need to do more than build your franchise to get your customers to come. Just because you put that sign out front, it might take some time to build your customer base. Unless you're opening a McDonald's, you will most likely be helping to build the brand you just bought. The difference between a franchise and an independent business is that with a franchise, business owners are able to build upon an established brand versus one that is unknown. You have the track record of the larger franchise, you have the systems, you have some level of brand recognition, but if you don't know how to go out there and sell the business, you are going to be disappointed in the outcomes.

From advertising to the grand opening to networking in your community, your job is to get out there and sell your business. You might be working in the business at night, but by day, you need to be out there, working on the business. You are its face and fiercest advocate.

No matter your product or service, your first job is to get out there and deliver it to your prospective customers. Of course, the franchisor should also be a part of these efforts, but ultimately, the success or failure of every franchise can be linked to whether the franchisee was willing to market the business from day one.

At Image One, we work with our franchisees to get their grand opening down, but once the doors open, the real work begins. It's doubtful the phone will be ringing off the hook or customers will be rushing through the door as soon as your business opens. You will be building the franchise brick by brick, even if it isn't brick and mortar.

Unless you're an experienced franchisee, you will go through an enormous transition in the beginning. Even if you're switching from an independent company to a franchise, there is going to be a learning curve. Though you might be used to the entrepreneurial side of the business, you are going to be learning a new system and bureaucracy. Things are going to move more slowly, and many times the franchisor is going to have a different opinion than you. Unfortunately, it's their opinion that counts most.

For someone moving from W-2 life, the changes can be even more dramatic. Not only are you negotiating a new system, you're also learning how to run your own business. This can take you far out of your comfort zone, and though that may be exciting for some, there are definitely a lot of terrifying moments in the process. Both one of the benefits and the challenges is that you aren't punching a time clock anymore. If you need somebody to tell you it is time to get out of bed and go to work, you need to keep working for somebody else. Being self-employed isn't for everybody. If you don't have the motivation to do what needs to be done every day without somebody looking over your shoulder, you may not want to move in that direction. If, on the other hand, you are the type of person who goes in early, stays late, and makes sure all of the work is done before you leave for the day, you are wasting precious time working for somebody else. Find the franchise that is a good fit, take the plunge, and get started on that ROY.

Being a franchisee requires a number of key traits, but it boils down to personality as much as it does pocketbook.

If you have the skills and the drive, finding the financing shouldn't be as hard as it sounds. It's all about learning how to leverage your most important asset—you—in order to achieve an ROI and ROY that makes all the hard work, long days, late nights, and financial investment worth your time.

There's a quote from Dan Sullivan: "Courage isn't the absence of fear; it's being afraid and doing what you know needs to be done anyway."

One should approach franchising with a reasonable amount of fear, but being afraid doesn't mean you should give up on your dream. All it means is that you need to do even more due diligence. Your success depends on your research.

You are entering into what will likely be a 10-year agreement with a franchisor that will touch every area of your life—from finances to family to professional and personal values. You are making a commitment to the franchise, but first, you need to make the commitment to yourself, your family, and to the people and institutions who will help you finance the franchise. That commitment includes doing research, making the right choices, and following the system so you can see the business succeed. If you can, the rewards will be well worth the investment.

Chapter Six:
What's Next, Tim?

I hope by now you are well on your way to thinking about the different franchise opportunities available; finding the right franchise for your budget, qualifications, and personal interests; and determining what kind of industry you might be interested in. Perhaps you have even completed some initial research on the subject.

If franchising is right for you, I firmly believe you will find the right franchise.

Not only do you want to find a quality franchise that has long-term viability, you also want to find one for which you are qualified. It's great if your passion is poké bowls, but if you don't have the resources to open in the hottest trend in quick-service restaurants, it won't matter how much you love raw salmon.

Once you are able to establish the business structure and industry that best fit your abilities and finances, it's time to find your franchise, which is a little like finding your spouse.

It is no easy task. Finding your fit isn't just about interest and/or qualifications, it's also about finding a company you respect, people you want to work with, and a business culture in line with your personal and professional values. It's also about finding a franchise that wants you.

There is an old story about a guy who was searching for the perfect woman to marry. When he finally found her, she wasn't interested because she was busy looking for the perfect man. There is no 100% perfect fit. You will find fault in every franchise, just like you will find fault in every person and that person can find fault in you. You need to find one that meets your criteria, and move forward from there.

If a franchise is like a marriage, this is the part where you need to start dating—and yes, that can be as awkward and disappointing as actual dating. At least that's what I remember from the late '80s before I met my wife Maria; there was no disappointment there.

Looking for the right franchise is pretty much the same thing. You will consider some potential partners you think will be a great fit, but they won't feel the same way about you, and you will part ways. You will look at others and think, "Wow, who could ever partner with them? That person is unbearable!" You will find others who seem appealing at first, but the more you get to know them, the more you'd rather just be friends—or, in the case of franchising, just a customer. Don't be discouraged; just like they say that there is somebody for everybody, there is a franchise for everybody too. If you are really struggling to figure it out, contact a broker or consultant for help.

You're going to want to meet with the franchisors you are considering. Even if it's over the phone or video conference, you need to get to know them. This courtship period might last only a couple of weeks or it might last several months, but in that time, your job is to determine whether these are people with whom you can establish a healthy, long-term relationship.

You're going to want to make sure that this is the fit you've been seeking.

Find Your Franchise

Let's say you decide you're interested in opening a frozen yogurt shop. There are plenty of options out there, and all require relatively the same level of investment. The real decision boils down to which one is the right fit for you.

As you start to investigate specific franchises, here are some key factors to consider:

- **Total investment required**—This includes franchise fees, training expenses, costs for leasehold improvements or real estate, employees, inventory, marketing, furniture and fixtures, and equipment.

- **Ongoing costs**—Keep in mind that there are royalty and marketing/advertising fees on top of your regular operational expenses.

- **Training and support**—Find out what training and support are provided by the franchisors, if you will be charged for these, and how much it will cost, as well as where the training will take place.

- **Competition**—Research how close other franchises are to your location and if there are any existing businesses already competing.

Once you've assessed your own budget and net worth; your experience, skills, and personal interests; and have set a timeline for your goals, you can begin to start "dating." Like romance, the perfect franchise is one that best suits your skills, interests, and budget.

But where do you start?

As I have mentioned, there are franchise expos all across the country several times a year, representing all the major markets. Before you go, make sure you do your homework. The people who walk in overwhelmed are the ones who don't know where to start. The franchise fair shouldn't be your introduction to franchising, but rather a networking space in which to introduce yourself to the franchises you believe might be a good fit.

If you are interested in frozen yogurt, then a franchise fair would be a great place to meet some franchises working in your area. You can meet their team and see what they have to offer. You'll want to see who you connect with personally as well as which franchise provides the right financial and professional fit.

If you go to a franchise expo unsure of what you're looking for, you might never go back. You'll end up with a name badge that's been scanned by 200 booths, a bag full of brochures, and about two years' worth of follow-up phone calls and emails from franchisors.

I love franchise expos. I go to them all the time. But I also know that potential franchisees need to do their homework before they walk into the room.

As we discussed, *Entrepreneur* puts out a list of top franchises every February.

In addition, www.franchisebusinessreview.com offers third-party reviews; it's like the Yelp of franchising. They rate the top 50 franchises in different categories, from home-based to tech to low-cost to veteran-oriented.

Speaking of veterans, a great resource for our military members is the International Franchise Association's VetFran program, which is devoted to helping veterans obtain franchises. Through VetFran, veterans can access exclusive discounts and benefits and connect with some 0% financing programs. For a lot of veterans, franchising is great transition back into civilian life. Because they're accustomed to working within a structured system, vets typically follow a process to the letter, which is especially helpful in franchising.

I also recommend that you find any filed reviews or complaints by visiting the Better Business Bureau.

Also check out Unhappy Franchisee at www.unhappyfranchisee.com to read reviews from existing franchisees and customers.

Finally, if you're looking for an easy search engine for franchise opportunities, FranchiseGator.com lists franchise opportunities across the country.

Check out these links and other resources on www.TimsFranchiseBook.com.

Are You a Fit for Them?

As we've discussed, it's important that you know everything you need to about the franchise. But the other half of the franchise decision is whether or not you are a good match for the franchise.

Franchisors typically set minimum requirements to make sure that franchisees are qualified. Requirements vary significantly depending on the franchisors and the type of franchise you're buying, but they often include:

- **Credit score**—Generally, a score of 680 or higher is ideal, but some franchisors might overlook a lower number.

- **Net worth**—If your franchise requires a large initial investment, you'll need to have a higher net worth in order to qualify.

- **Cash**—You need to have enough cash to either cover the franchise costs or at least a down payment if financing is involved.

- **Other income**—Since you won't be earning immediate income from the franchise, you will need other forms of income or savings to maintain your lifestyle while establishing the franchise.

- **Industry experience**—Although some franchises do not require industry-related background, franchisors often prefer to see a franchisee with some relevant experience.

- **Management experience**—Since most franchises involve managing a team and/or business, franchisors will often expect you to have similar experience on your resume.

- **Timeline**—Though not a requirement, this is also a good time to draft your timeline for buying a franchise, including how long it will take to select a franchisor, review franchise disclosure documents and franchise agreements, obtain financing, and choose a location.

Don't be dissuaded if you're not a perfect candidate. Few people are. Be sure to speak with the franchisor when you seem to lack the abilities or capabilities required and see if they might be willing to overlook any deficits or help you strengthen your areas of expertise that might be required for the job.

Do Your Due Diligence

As I've mentioned, once you find a franchise you like, your job is to get to know them as well as possible before you sign on the dotted line.

You can do a lot of homework yourself by Googling the brand, the industry (to study trends), and the franchisor. You should check out regulators' websites. Review the franchisor's financial condition. Their audited financials will give you a good picture. Ultimately, the best way to know how a franchise works is to visit them.

Don't just call them; actually go to the business to see how it feels. And I'm not talking about just visiting the franchisor's office; visit one of the franchisee's locations, or even a couple of them if there are several in your area. By visiting different locations, you can get a sense of whether the business is running well and its employees are happy.

The next step is to fill out the franchisor's preliminary questionnaire and application forms. The preliminary application helps franchisors eliminate any franchisees who don't qualify.

It's recommended that you fill out these initial forms completely and accurately to help the franchisors best assess your abilities and capabilities. Assuming you meet the franchisor's initial requirements, you will likely set a meeting with the franchisor's representative and get a copy of the FDD.

Once you receive the FDD (which we will discuss in depth shortly), begin making those phone calls to their previous franchisees. As I mentioned, the franchisor will frequently circle a few, but you should also call the ones the franchisor didn't circle, as well as the ones who aren't in the franchise system anymore. Find out why they left. Remember an existing franchisee might be bound not to say anything about a dispute with the franchisor. He or she might have signed a confidentiality agreement at the end of a mediation. Don't passively accept everything you are told. That said, just because one franchisee had a bad experience doesn't mean you should count the franchise out. We've all had our disputes and disagreements. If eight or nine out of 10 calls are positive, then you're probably safe to move forward. But if you're hearing the same complaints or issues from multiple franchisees, past and present, take heed.

Below is a great checklist to use as you are considering a franchise. See how they score and how various franchises stack up against one another.

THE FRANCHISE ORGANIZATION	1	2	3
Does the franchisor have a good record?			
Do the franchise leaders have relevant experience?			
Do the franchisor and franchisees have proof of profitability?			
Are industry sales strong?			
Is the product or service competitively priced?			
Are exclusive territories offered?			
How successful are franchises in this area?			
Are the fees and royalties reasonable?			
How attractive are the renewal and termination conditions?			
Does the franchisor help with the site selection and lease negotiation?			
Is the training program robust and effective?			
Does the franchisor provide financing?			
Are manuals, sales kits, accounting systems, and purchasing guides provided?			
Does the franchisor sponsor an advertising fund?			

Before you move forward, do your due diligence on your own abilities as well. Connect with an accountant to make sure you're in the right financial space to move forward. Run the projections on your anticipated expenses and profits and determine whether you are financially viable to invest. Also, check in with a franchise attorney. Don't call your Uncle John who practices family law. You will want to work with a franchise attorney who can help you to review the FDD and other legal documents.

Remember, don't rely on any one source of information. There is always going to be another franchise opportunity. There is no reason to rush into buying a franchise. Franchisors want satisfied and successful franchisees just as much as you want to run a happy and profitable franchise.

Cultural Connection

After doing your self-assessment and initial research, you should narrow down your options to a few franchises that best suit your preferences and budget.

Before you fill out the application, you need to make sure you get along.

Remember, once you make a decision to sign a franchise agreement, you are about to enter into a five or 10-year agreement, one which takes considerable time, energy, and money to join—and even more to prematurely exit.

When I joined the master franchise in Chicago, it seemed like it was a good fit on every level. Over the next few years, however, as my partner and I began to grow and expand the business, it became clear that we were no longer a good fit as a master franchisor in that organization. We decided it made more sense for us to go out on our own.

Now, we were at the end of our term, but franchise agreements can be incredibly entangled. You are developing a business using someone else's systems, logo, branding, and intellectual property. To attempt to continue elements of the same business under a new guise can be challenging, and extremely expensive, as my partner and I found out. Even though we were at the end of our term, the litigation against us lasted longer and cost us more than most divorces.

If you invest in that frozen yogurt company, you're going to find that leaving the franchise and opening a frozen yogurt shop of your own can be complicated, sometimes impossible. Your franchise agreement will likely have a non-compete to prevent you from going out and competing with the brand during and even after the term of the agreement—as well it should. Such a provision is included to protect you and all the franchisees in the system, as well as the brand and the franchisor.

You want to make sure your franchisor is the right partner, someone you would trust to be with in a deep and honest relationship.

But beyond the personalities, the company itself needs to be a fit. If the way it does business doesn't resemble how you do business, you will most likely butt heads. And if you butt heads on day one, things won't get much better by year five.

You don't need to become best friends with the people you're about to start working with (it's probably better that you don't), but you should have a mutual respect and a professional connection. At the end of the day, you should like them.

Liking them can take you pretty far, especially when things get challenging—and they will always get challenging.

You can train for a skill; you can't train to change someone's personality.

If you've done your due diligence and walk out of meetings looking forward to working with the team; if you share a corporate, cultural, and professional belief system; if you like each other and can see a partnership that will strengthen over time, then you have just made your decision. You have found the franchise that fits.

I do want to spend some time discussing partnerships. This applies both to your franchisor as well as any investors who might be helping you with the business. First, be clear about your expectations at the outset. The more people know and understand their roles in the partnership, the fewer opportunities there are for confusion and disagreement. With your franchisor, the franchise agreement will spell out in detail virtually everything that is expected of you as a franchisee—and virtually everything you should expect from the franchisor. A partnership in your franchise with a friend or family member needs to have everything spelled out as well.

I had the wonderful opportunity to partner with a colleague for nearly 20 years, and I can say that in all those years, we got along 99% of the time. We are both very different people with very different skill sets, but we knew what to expect from one another, and because of that, we were both able to successfully hold up our respective ends of the partnership. We complemented each other in business—his abilities were different than mine, and mine were different from his—but we each knew what our role was in the day-to-day operations of the business. We respected each other's opinions, roles, and value. Unfortunately, many partnerships are not so successful.

Over the years, I have seen several partnerships end in disaster. The hardest of these are frequently those built between friends or family members who find themselves in situations they never imagined would occur in their partnership. Most of the time, disputes arise when the members of the partnership have different expectations on profit distribution or how work should be divided. Tensions grow until they reach a boiling point and we end up with a big mess to clean up. Many partnerships don't survive past this point. That results in one partner buying out the other, which can get messy too. If there isn't a clear exit strategy, or a partner doesn't have the financial wherewithal to buy out the business, it can mean the sale of the franchise as well as the termination of the partnership. Frequently, there is an additional consequence: the end of a friendship.

I had a very successful partnership that lasted nearly 20 years until my business partner decided it was time to retire. I don't ever tell people not to have a partner, but I do recommend proceeding with caution. Make sure all parties involved understand what their role is in the partnership and spell it out in writing. Confirm that everybody understands who is getting paid for what, and what profit distributions will look like. You should even include an exit plan: what happens if somebody wants to exit the partnership or if somebody exits unexpectedly because of illness or death? These are things we don't talk about until we need to, which is often too late.

The Franchise Disclosure Document

The Franchise Disclosure Document rule originated as a consumer protection tool. The document is required by the Federal Trade Commission (FTC) and consists of 23 items that follow a specified format and order. The document's quality and content will vary from franchisor to franchisor, but it is typically a 100+ page document that outlines your responsibilities as a franchisee, the fees you need to pay, and the rules and regulations you need to follow. Additionally, it outlines the legal obligations of the franchisor to the franchisee. It also includes information about the franchisor, such as its financial and legal history. Getting an FDD will give you much of the information you need to know before deciding if the potential franchise is a fit.

Franchisors are mandated by the FTC to provide prospective franchisees with an FDD at least 14 days before any agreements are signed and any payments are made. No agreements can be signed during that 14-day break, which is considered a "cooling off" period. During that time, franchisees are advised to read and review the FDD carefully. All FDDs follow the same format, but the level of disclosure and transparency may vary greatly between franchisors.

There are 23 items that are required to be in a specific order, no matter the franchise opportunity.

Item 1: The Franchisor, Parents, Predecessors and Affiliates: This section provides the background information about the franchisor, and any connection with other companies that you need to be made aware of, as well as the business opportunity they are offering.

Item 2: Business Experience: This section simply explains what experience the individuals who run the company have so that you understand their qualifications.

Item 3: Litigation: This section includes any pending or concluded litigation that involves the franchise system and is required to be disclosed to the prospective franchisees.

Item 4: Bankruptcy: If there has been a bankruptcy related to the franchisor and the disclosure is required, it will be contained in this section.

Item 5: Initial Fees: This section contains the information about the initial franchise fee you will be required to pay the franchisor. It will also include information about financing options and veterans' programs, as well as conversion programs, if they apply.

Item 6: Other Fees: This section will include required royalty payments, advertising fund requirements, and any other fees you will be required to pay to the franchisor.

Item 7: Estimated Initial Investment: This section will give you an estimate of the total cost to open your franchise. It will include the initial franchise fee, plus the cost of necessary equipment, supplies, license registrations, travel expenses, a vehicle, lease payments, and any other cost that the franchisor believes is likely to be incurred in the opening of your franchise. This will often be presented as a low-high range.

Item 8: Restrictions on Sources of Products and Services: Your franchisor can sell you required goods and services as long as they disclose to you that they are making money on the sales, as well as the amount of revenue from required purchases.

Item 9: Franchisee's Obligations: This section will list your principal obligations under the franchise agreement and any other agreements.

Item 10: Financing: If a franchisor offers financing, it will be detailed in this section.

Item 11: The Franchisor's Assistance, Advertising, Computer Systems and Training: This section will detail the franchisor's obligations to you, as well as the requirements placed on you related to these items.

Item 12: Territory: If your franchisor offers a protected territory, it will be explained here.

Item 13: Trademarks: This section will list any trademarks that the franchisor utilizes in the franchise. It will explain how the use of such trademarks is granted to the franchisee, as well as if there is any interference in using said trademarks.

Item 14: Patents, Copyrights, and Proprietary Information: This section will explain the use of any

Patents, Copyrights and Proprietary Information that are owned by the Franchisor.

Item 15: Obligation to Participate in the Actual Operation of the Franchise Business: Some franchise systems require that you personally participate in the day-to-day operation of the franchise. Other systems will allow you to simply purchase the franchise and hire people to run the operation on your behalf.

Item 16: Restrictions on What the Franchise Can Sell: The products and services that you can sell are generally restricted to those items approved by the franchisor. If you want to sell a product or provide a service outside of the approved items, you would need approval in writing from the franchisor.

Item 17: Renewal, Termination, Transfer and Dispute Resolution: This section will outline the length of the agreement, what happens at the end of the term and your right for renewal, as well as what your options are for transferring (selling) your franchise, the explanation of how and why your franchise could be terminated, and finally, a description of the dispute resolution, such as an arbitration board.

Item 18: Public Figures: If the system uses a public figure such as a professional athlete to promote the franchise, it must be disclosed here.

Item 19: Financial Performance Representations: This is an optional section that is becoming more common. The FTC Rule allows franchisors to use information from existing franchised units, including company owned units, to show the actual or potential financial performance of existing units, provided that there is reasonable basis for inclusion in Item 19. The information in this section will vary greatly from system to system. There is no specified data to be included. It is solely based on the franchisor's discretion. Most FDDs don't include information on the average franchise business performance, average unit volume (AUV), and typical profit/loss, but if they do, it will be included here.

Item 20: Outlets and Franchisee Information: This section consists of a number of tables that outline the number of units that have been opened, closed, and continued to operate in the past three years. This section will give you an understanding of the growth and stability of the franchise system. Additionally, there are exhibits that include the names, addresses, and phone numbers of all existing franchisees, as well as those that left the system in the last 12 months.

Item 21: Financial Statements: The franchisor is required to provide audited financial statements for three years.

Item 22: Contracts: This section contains an exhibit which represents the franchise agreement you will sign. It may be the actual agreement if there are no changes to it. It will also include other agreements that may be applicable, such as a veterans' incentive or a conversion addendum if you are already running a business in the industry that you are converting to the franchise system.

Item 23: Receipts: You will find two sets of receipts in the back of the FDD, one to be kept for your records and another to be returned to the franchisor. Because of the 14-day rule, you should NOT mark the receipt with any date other than the date that you actually received the FDD.

The FDD contains a great deal of information, and that is why it is generally over 100 pages. Some, including Image One's, are well over 200 pages (ours is actually 218 pages this year). I always joke that if you can't sleep, pick up the FDD—it is sure to cure insomnia! The FDD isn't intended to be interesting reading; however, it is a legal document designed to outline the responsibilities of the franchise partnership. The FTC Rule is very clear about what can be included, and there is no room for fluff, sales, or marketing information to try to sway your opinion. It is strictly a legal document that was developed with the intent to protect the consumer.

In addition, FDDs will not offer reasons for unit closures or industry comparisons. The FDD is a legal document that must follow a specific format as outlined by the FTC. In some states, known as registration states, the FDD is reviewed and approved by a state agency as well. If you research the franchisor's press releases, annual reports, and public filings, you may well be able to find more information. Another great third-party resource is <u>FRANdata</u>, which offers more specific financials on franchises where available. Typically, any lenders or external investors will also want to see the FDD.

As a quick review, here are some common types of information you will find in the FDD:

- The franchise system's size and three-year growth trends

- The franchise's brand presence in the prospect's state

- The franchisor's leadership team and their experience

- Initial investment, one-time fees, and potential ongoing charges

- Support offered to the franchises (e.g. training, financing, operational assistance)

- The franchisor's financial performance

Since the FDD informs so much of your business plan, it is important that you understand it thoroughly. As I mentioned, it's well worth hiring an attorney who specializes in franchising to help you read through the disclosure agreement and other legal documents. He or she will be able to walk you through the language and flag anything that feels out of place in the documents.

There is little opportunity to make changes to the franchise agreement, but if you feel like something isn't right, or if there is some room to negotiate, this is the time to discuss it.

Discovery Day

Discovery Day, or "Meet the Team" Day, typically takes places in the franchisor's corporate office and is the ideal opportunity for a potential franchisee to get to know the franchise and its management team. This is not only an opportunity to learn more about the company culture and the individual personalities of the people you'll be working with, but also for both franchisor and potential franchisee to ask questions about anything that will affect the success of the business. It's also the time to voice concerns outside of those addressed in the FDD. Many times, a Discovery

Day will include lunch or dinner outside of the office so that franchisors and franchisees can get to know each other even better.

A Discovery Day's typical agenda involves group presentations, one-on-one meetings and interviews, and possibly even visits to existing franchise locations. Try to look out for possible red flags during Discovery Day, which include the following:

- Personality or cultural clashes

- Disorganization at the corporate level

- Promises or assurances that are not put in writing, especially something that varies from what is written in the FDD

- Questions that are not answered directly

- Concerns that are not addressed clearly

- Hard sells

In the end, always trust your gut. If something doesn't feel right, it likely means something is wrong. Finally, try to learn more about the business's growth plans. Another red flag to watch out for is how fast the business intends to grow. If the company is trying to expand too quickly, their growth might not be sustainable, and could create chaos for your business before it even opens. On the other hand, a company that has no growth plans could limit a franchisee's success.

Discovery Day is also time for the franchisor to ask questions that aren't addressed in your application. Aside from making sure that you meet their specific qualifications, a franchisor will also evaluate your level of commitment and enthusiasm for their business. They'll want to know if you're willing to follow their rules and policies and are a good fit for them.

The Franchise Agreement

The franchise agreement is the formal contract that establishes the relationship between the franchisor and the franchisee. This contract gives you the legal right to own and open a franchise under its rules and regulations.

If the franchisor made verbal promises or deals during your meeting, it's important these items are included in the contract. Whether it's a promise to provide legal advisement, marketing efforts, or other training or advertising support, all of these expectations should be included in the agreement. In addition, the contract should include rules on suppliers, pricing, transfer of ownership, protection of territory, royalty fees, hiring staff, training, and other relevant support.

You must address any discrepancies between what was discussed and what is in the contract, because once you sign, you are agreeing to the terms of the relationship as set forth in the agreement. There might be opportunities for amendments, but franchisors will more often insist on what is in the contract.

There are no guarantees in anything in life, especially in partnerships. As in all business endeavors (and life), those who take the risks get the rewards. As much as a franchise might feel like a perfect fit, as much as you might love the industry or the franchisor, you are still taking a leap. You should have done enough research that you're not afraid to look down. You must know the strengths and weaknesses of your new partner. And you must know your own.

Huge companies have come and gone. Never in a million years did people think Sears or Toys R Us would go through so much turmoil, for example. The risk is there for us all, but who better to bet on than yourself? Just as there is a Return on You, there is also risk—not just for you but for the business you are investing in as well.

You are your own best asset. By connecting with the right franchise, you can leverage your skills, talent, and energy to build a successful business. At the end of the day, you are the biggest factor in your own success.

To learn more about the franchising process, visit www.TimsFranchiseBook.com.

Chapter Seven: Launch Your Franchise

So you've found the right franchise. You've done your due diligence and signed the franchise agreement. After months, even years of waiting, you've made the plunge into franchising.

Congratulations! Now, it's time for the fun to begin.

For a lot of people, this is where the rubber meets the road. Most of what has happened before this point was training season. We are now in the game, and every decision you make moving forward will ultimately determine the success of your business.

Here is the thing about failure. When things go south, you can point your finger in all directions, but ultimately, you will be the one responsible. The harsh reality is that everything that happens in your life is because of your actions or inactions. If you are single, happily married, or divorced, it is because you have caused it to be that way. If you have $1,000 or $100,000 in the bank, you are the reason. No matter what the situation, you have had a hand in creating your success or failure.

Now, I understand that things happen to people that are completely out of their control. Sometimes people are in car accidents or suffer great health setbacks. That is not their fault, but how they respond to those situations is certainly within their control. You can sit back and claim you've been dealt a bad hand, or you can adapt and push forward harder than before. It is all about attitude, and your attitude is 100% up to you. We all make mistakes from time to time. When you do, own up to them, take responsibility for your actions, and fix the situation.

My biggest mistake occurred when I was a good 10 years into my business. I had failed to appropriately pay my payroll taxes and the IRS caught up with me. As the gentleman at my front door kindly informed me, I owed the IRS $100,000 in back taxes. That visit to my front door was the single scariest moment of my life. Basically, I had been using the IRS as my credit line and had put myself in a position to lose everything in the process.

Sure, I wanted to blame other people. I wanted to act naïve or confused. I was angry at the IRS, but the fact was, I was the one responsible for my company, and I was now the one responsible for the consequences. Over the next few years, I worked to pay off Uncle Sam, the world's worst loan shark.

Once the debt was paid, I realized I had learned a major lesson, and like most lessons, it had to cost me something. I learned early in business that there is no losing. There is winning and there is learning. This was clearly a learning situation, and it was a good lesson to learn—expensive, but good. When you are in business, you will realize that sometimes you have to pay tuition to learn from your mistakes. It really isn't any different than paying for college. It's just more of a self-study program than a traditional education offers.

When we run our own business, there is no CEO to blame but ourselves. We are the CEO. Which is why from day one, you are responsible for making the best decisions under whatever set of circumstances you might be facing, even if, *especially* if, they're not favorable to your success.

That can be even trickier when you are operating as a franchisee, because so much of the decision-making is no longer under your control.

Prior to becoming a franchisee, you had the opportunity to make your own decisions and determine the terms of your agreements; now, a lot of your business is being directed by your franchisor.

The best way to succeed is to listen and learn.

If this is your first franchise, the learning curve is going to be steep, and you're going to need all the help you can get. Don't be afraid to reach out to your franchisor for help. Ask the dumb questions. My mom always told me that there is no such thing as a dumb question. If you don't know something, simply ask. Some of the dumbest questions I have ever asked led to the wisest answers. Usually a dumb question isn't a dumb question at all, it's just the one that everyone else is afraid to ask. Don't be afraid to say, "I don't know."

When I am working with a new franchisee, I can tell right away whether that person will be successful based on how many questions they ask. If they come to me with a page of questions in their notebook, I know there is a good chance they're going to do fine.

If they start the franchise thinking they already know everything, chances are they're going to struggle with franchise culture.

Moving forward, it is both your business and the business of the franchise brand. As you begin to build your business, you have to keep that partnership in mind every step of the way. They are there to help you. The best thing you can do is let them.

Have a Road Map for Where You Want to Go

You know you're working with the right franchisor when they want to support your overall goals. Before you determine what your next steps are, figure out where you want to go, and how you want to get there. Start from retirement and work backwards. What do you want your career to look like, starting today and ending when you finally hang up your boots? Take a look at the grand plan for your business and ask yourself about where you want to be in five years:

- Do you want to open multiple locations?

- Do you want to expand locally or regionally?

- What would it take to get there?

- What kind of marketing or advertising do you anticipate you'll want or need?

- What do you expect will be your staff growth?

- What are the deadlines for your goals? A goal without a deadline is simply a dream!

You can't just say you're going to open up a business someday because someday isn't a day of the week. You want to put a timeline on each individual goal. If you don't have a deadline, it's going to be hard to get started. Write it down. I am going to accomplish X in three months, Y in six months, and Z in 18 months.

Most people don't write down their goals, but successful people do. It's what sets them apart from those who struggle to achieve their dreams. Years ago, I took a course on goal setting from Brian Tracy. In one of the program's exercises, we were asked to write down 100 goals. That was a difficult task, but I did it, and then I forgot about it until about a year ago, when I came across the list in a junk drawer. It had been about 10 years, and guess what? 63 of the 100 goals had been achieved!

From minor things to major things, simply writing down the goals helped to keep them in my mind, even if I wasn't actively looking at the list every day. In the end, I was amazed by how many goals I had accomplished.

After I shared the list with my wife, Maria, we adjusted some of the goals on the old list that weren't relevant anymore, and we put together a new list.

What are your goals? Personal, professional, business, family, spiritual…anything. Could you write down 100 of them? I know it sounds challenging, but once you start realizing how much you want to achieve, it's easy to find the motivation. There is a lot to get done and only one life (that we know of) in which to accomplish it all.

Make a concrete plan and share that with your franchisor. Just as your goal is to help them be successful, their goal should be to help you. Together, you should be making the right decisions from day one to support your road map and help get you where you want to be. Having the right franchise means the franchisor and franchisee are helping one another to reach their goals.

Get the Right Financing

If you think you are going to need financing, it's never too early to start looking. Your franchise fee is due at the time that you execute the franchise agreement. Depending on the franchise you select, you may also need funds for equipment, a buildout, or other start-up expenses.

You need a strong and convincing business plan, including years of growth projections, if you intend to borrow funds for your franchise. It's important to address things in your business plan that are not included in the franchise disclosure document, such as your franchise location's potential revenues, startup and normal operating expenses, and cost of financing. You can find many business plan templates online or work with a professional to turn that road map, your FDD, and your franchisor's growth strategy, into a living document.

Every franchise has different funding requirements. If you need funds for new, ground-up construction or to lease a space for your new franchise, make sure you closely coordinate with the franchisor and your potential lender since they might have certain rules about the location. You might need their approval before you start building or renovating your space.

If the franchise requires a significant investment in equipment, the franchisor will likely recommend a distributor or wholesaler. They might also offer financing, which will typically be structured as a lease and have a term of up to five years.

In most cases, lenders will not loan you money to cover the franchising fee. However, your franchising fee can be part of your down payment for an SBA or conventional bank loan. As briefly discussed before, you can also consider any of the other following funding options:

- Rollover for Business Startups (ROBS)—If you have at least $50,000 in a qualified retirement account, you can use it to fund your franchise without having to pay early withdrawal penalties and taxes. A ROBS is not a loan, doesn't require lender approval, and is typically faster than most startup loans.

- SBA Loan—SBA loans are guaranteed by the government and have low interest rates, making them one of the best options to fund a business. Requirements for SBA loans can be strict (typically, you'll need a credit score of 680+ and a 20% down payment), which makes it more difficult for new businesses to qualify.

- Bank Loan—Conventional bank loans are sometimes more difficult to qualify for when compared to SBA loans because they are not guaranteed by the government. However, if you have a strong credit history, a high net worth, and existing business dealings with the bank, you might qualify.

- Financing from franchisor—Some franchisors offer financing to help fund all or a portion of the franchise costs.

- Partner lenders—You can also partner with a financial investor who will work to cover the financial expenses of the business as you manage the front-end operations. Again, these partner-ships can be extremely successful, but if the expectations are not clearly outlined, they can also be incredibly stressful.

- Friends and family—When possible, friends and family might be good options, but again, you will want to be clear about your needs, expectations, and deliverables. When does your family expect to see their money back? Are they anticipating interest? Even if the funds are coming from a parent or sibling, draw up an investor agreement so that everyone is on the same page.

Finally, make sure to consider your cash flow for the next few years before you agree to short-term loans. Longer term loans are preferable since recurring payments will be lower and it can help make your first few years easier. Make sure your financing is sustainable. You don't want to go underwater on a business by presuming it will make more than it does, or end up with a predatory loan. Just as you have done your due diligence on the franchising, do your due diligence on your financing.

Choose a Location

If your franchise is not home-based or mobile, you need to choose a location where you can run your business. Franchisors will likely provide you with guidelines so you meet their location requirements. They may require anything from a certain distance from other franchises to a certain number of parking spots, so work with a commercial real estate agent to help you find a location that meets the franchisor's requirements.

If you expect to be in the same location for seven or more years and you have the capital, you may want to consider buying the building. Just keep in mind, you might find it more difficult to qualify for a commercial loan from a conventional lender. Most franchises prefer to lease property initially as it requires less money upfront and is less risky.

If you're leasing a property, consider the safety and accessibility of your location. For retail, you will want to make sure the area is appropriate for your community and target customers. Also, estimate the square footage you need as accurately as possible and negotiate your rent without extending your lease longer than necessary. For office spaces, consider the location of your employees, clients, and other specific business needs. It's always a good idea to get an attorney to review any potential lease before you sign on the dotted line.

Trainings

Before you open the business, you and your staff should participate in significant training with the franchisor. This might feel like you're drinking from a firehose, but outside of the brand, the training and systems are the biggest piece of your investment. Your franchisor's job is to offer all the necessary trainings and workshops to equip you and your staff with the skills and knowledge necessary to run your business. If for any reason your franchise doesn't offer trainings, you might need to consider another franchisor.

The training sessions will either take place in their headquarters, at a franchise location, or online. They usually last one to two weeks.

Typical training sessions will cover everything you need to know, including the franchise's products and services, the systems you'll be using, and the policies and guidelines you need to put in place. Some franchisors offer trainings in marketing, negotiating with suppliers, hiring and managing employees, filing permits, bookkeeping, creating reports, and more. These sessions will likely combine classroom lessons, hands-on work, and on-site training with equipment and systems.

You won't remember everything from the trainings, but the information should be in your operations manual. Also, your franchisor should continue to offer ongoing support where you can connect with other franchisees and reach out to the franchisor when you have questions or need help.

Time to Open

Once you have completed all the necessary training and your location is ready, the next step is to open for business. The franchisor should provide support for the actual opening of your franchise, which will mostly be centered on marketing and promotion to build your customer base.

If you have a retail operation, the grand opening will likely take place at the location. Many franchises have a soft opening to introduce themselves to the community before they are officially up and running. Also, most businesses allocate a portion of their first-year marketing budget to promote the grand opening.

For at-home or service-based businesses, it will be a far quieter affair. You might have a ribbon cutting at the franchisor's corporate office or at the local Chamber of Commerce. Either way, you will want to develop a fun and creative way to introduce your business to the community. In addition, reach out to other franchisees and your franchisor to find out what has been successful in the past.

Buying a franchise does not take the risk out of starting a business, but if you find the right franchise for you, review the FDD and franchise agreement carefully, and obtain the right financing, you'll be on the path to a successful business.

If it's business-to-business, you're going to be hitting the ground running doing sales. If it's a restaurant or that frozen yogurt shop, you're going to be busy making sure your customers are happy and spreading the word about your business.

The hard work might begin the day you open, but as anyone who has opened a business will tell you, it's also the most exciting part. It is the honeymoon stage to your new marriage and though you might just be getting to know your franchisor, as long as you are honest, humble, and always come prepared with questions, this should be a fun and exciting time in your business (if also the most stressful).

I remember when my first business really got moving. Some days I would literally work 24-36 hours straight to get a job done (thankfully, I was young, so I could handle it). But even then, I often felt like I had just played a game of basketball or football—all four quarters without a single break! Just like when you hit the gym, the work will feel good because you are building something: your future. When your muscles hurt, you know you're getting a positive result. When you don't feel the burn, you're not building any muscle.

And for that first year or two, you are going to be building your franchise muscle, and every day, you're going to learn more. With that, you will also be building the relationship with your franchisor. You will be getting to know one another, and though there will be ups and downs, you will probably find it to be one of the most important, and often rewarding, relationships in your life.

Chapter Eight:
Secrets to Success

You did it. And now, you're learning how to succeed while doing it.

As I said at the beginning of the book, the best part of owning a franchise is that you're in business for yourself, but not in business by yourself. You have a support system in place for a reason: you are paying for it. It's like having a warranty on your car. When something goes wrong, are you going to access your warranty, or are you going to pay out of pocket for coverage you've already invested in?

Your franchisor is the best warranty a business can have. They have been there before, they have made all the mistakes, and they are there to walk you through the questions and concerns.

Access your warranty. That is what it is for. Since you're not in business alone, it's not just a privilege to utilize your franchisor; it's a requirement. Why wouldn't you want to take advantage of the knowledge and experience your franchisor has? Don't be embarrassed if things aren't going exactly the way you planned. They rarely do. Adjust what you are doing and reach out to your franchisor for help.

If you are used to owning your own business, you will have to adjust to working from a different timetable, asking someone else for help, and getting permission. That can be awkward at first, but the payoff is you're sharing the risk.

You have a partner, which means you will have all the benefits and frustrations of partnership.

Now that you have your franchise up and running, how do you ensure its success? How do you build a healthy partnership with your franchisor?

How do you make sure you're building a strong enough foundation so you are able to expand (if that's in your five-year plan)?

How do you achieve that five-year plan?

The number one reason franchises fail (outside of choosing the wrong product or location) is that the franchisee doesn't build a strong allegiance with their franchisor. It is the main ingredient to success. But just as importantly, franchisees need to be willing to put in the time, money, effort, and commitment to seeing their business grow.

The only way the franchisor can be successful is if the franchisee is successful, and vice versa. So let's take a look at some of those secrets to success.

Engage Your Franchisor

From day one, you need to engage the franchisor. Ask for their support during your grand opening efforts and go to them as you encounter your first hurdles and accomplishments. They are a value-add as an investor. By treating them as such, you are building a strong foundation to what you hope will be a long and prosperous relationship. Remember, your franchisor has helped other franchisees to become successful. If they haven't, you are working with the wrong franchisor. Not only have they probably encountered the same issues you may be tackling, but they've probably also helped other franchisees through the process.

To ignore them in these early days is neither beneficial to you nor to the relationship.

Also, don't forget your fellow franchisees. Utilize their experience and ask for their opinions and help as needed. As you become a seasoned veteran in your franchise, don't ignore the new guy who may call you for help! Don't lose sight of the fact that YOU are the most important part of your franchise. It is you who needs to get up each day with an enthusiastic attitude to grow your business. Don't sit back and rely on others; get out there and do what you know needs to be done. You may not have the confidence to do everything at first, but that will come with time.

As I mentioned, I have been able to strengthen my own entrepreneurial skills by participating in Dan Sullivan's Strategic Coach program. In that program, Dan presented an exercise called the 4 Cs. It goes like this:

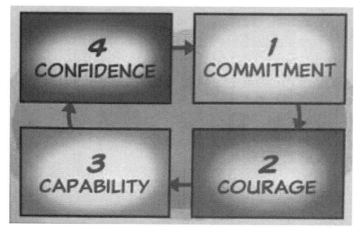

Courtesy of Strategic Coach, 2019.

First you need to make the commitment to do what needs to be done, then you need the courage to do it. After you do it for a while, you will develop the capability, which in turn leads to the confidence you need to succeed. This process starts over with every new commitment to a project or process you have never done before.

Some franchisees tend to forget that the success of one franchise benefits all the franchisees, not to mention the franchisor. You are in business together. You and the other franchisees are not in competition, you're in collaboration for the greater brand.

Your franchisor is there to support you with systems, processes, tools, product advice, and marketing because it is a shared relationship. You just bought the franchise for all those systems. Though you have some flexibility with the guidelines (as is the case with most, but not all, franchises), you should be using the system in which you just invested—not just as a support when you open your doors, but to help maintain your operations one, three, and 10 years down the road.

The best franchises are the ones who develop a community around their brand—the ones with 1-800 hotlines for franchisees, or those that cultivate a strong network between the franchise networks. But even if your franchisor doesn't have similar supports in place, you can always call them—or your fellow franchisees. You can help build that community.

Ultimately, your franchisor is there to help you run your business, sell your product, market the brand, and build the company's future. But again, the responsibility is still yours to make the business successful. Engage the franchisor to help you achieve that success.

Don't Expect to Get Rich Quick

If you think you're going to immediately get rich quick opening a franchise, you might want to close this book and go out and buy a lottery ticket. Like any business, franchises take time to build.

You need to connect to the local community. You need to find your customers and clients. You need to get over the learning curve inherent to any new business.

And you need to put in the hours to make all those things happen.

Sure, you have flexibility in a way that you don't with a 9-5. But you also need profit, which takes time and a whole lot of work.

If you have unrealistic expectations about franchising, or any business endeavor, you will most likely struggle. Just because you have the right brand or understand the systems doesn't mean you will immediately start making money in your sleep. As I mentioned, launching a business takes patience, patience, patience, which can ultimately lead to profit, profit, profit.

Reserves, Reserves, Reserves

Another issue with thinking you're going to get rich quick is that some people will run out of money or go negative because they have over-estimated initial profits or underestimated overhead costs associated with opening and running the franchise. When starting a franchise, it's always best to have a source of capital to go to if anything goes wrong with the first plan of action. Also, it is smart to have at least six months of operating reserves, including income to support your mortgage, car payments, kids' tuitions, and everything else.

The day you open, you're likely not going to be making enough money to create income. Some franchises will allow you to have a side income, so if you are able to segue from your former employment without a break, you might be in a better place. A lot of people, however, only have their reserves to sustain them.

Then there are all the ongoing costs we discussed when you're getting started. You need to ensure you're funded properly, even after the doors open.

Don't Expect Too Much from the Franchisor

We've spent a lot of time discussing how the franchisor is there to help you, but ultimately, it is your business, and you need to do what it takes to succeed. When someone "buys into" a franchise, there can be unrealistic expectations around what the franchisor is going to do for them. Though the franchisor is there to offer support, the business owner is still the one responsible for their success and their failure. Most franchisees' biggest mistake is believing that a franchisor will catch them when they're falling. Instead of looking at the franchisor as an ongoing support system, franchisees will treat them like 911, demanding help in times of crisis instead of developing the relationships and strategies to avert such crises in the first place.

The franchisees should be great entrepreneurs who are in partnership with the franchisor, not dependent on them. Because many of these franchises are templated, the support systems are designed to get a new franchisee up and running, not to actually build and run it. The new franchisee is tasked with acquiring new customers, not the franchisor. Franchisees will only be disappointed if they believe they can rely on the franchisor to draw in business for them. The franchisor is there to offer the systems; the franchisee's job is to make them work in order to engage customers and grow a successful business.

Be Willing to Give Up Some Control

If you are investing in a franchise system, be sure to use it. Nine times out of 10, when I meet someone who wasn't successful at franchising, it was because they didn't follow the template offered. If you can't follow the system, don't buy a franchise. Instead, look into becoming an independent business owner so you can build your own system.

There can be some wiggle room around the guidelines, and I always appreciate when businesses are able to tailor those guidelines to cultivate their own success, but you can't lose sight of the elements the franchise has perfected over the years. Sure, you might offer your employees benefits or options the franchisor doesn't always provide, but if you give them new uniforms, customers might be confused about the business they just entered. It's important that a customer can walk into any franchisee's property across the country and have the exact same experience—uniformity, in the end, is the key to good franchising.

The hardest part of being a franchisee is learning and adopting all the processes that exist in the brand you just bought.

Presumably, you chose your franchisor because you respected their best practices. If you have invested in a Little Caesar's, you're not going to start making customized pizzas. In order to be successful, franchisees need to embrace the system, which is why it is so important to find the system that works for you.

Expect the Unexpected

Lately, it seems like people keep predicting the next recession, only to see the economy climb. Yet history teaches us that the bust will come. It always does. That is the economic cycle—we go through times of expansion and retraction. There are always going to be good times and bad times, and you need to be prepared for how the bad times will affect your industry. If you are providing a service that people will hire in bad times, you can be a little less cautious in your thinking. The old saying is that there are two guarantees in life, but I believe there are three: death, dirt, and taxes. This means our business can handle blows to the economy, but when someone has to choose between letting go of employees or letting go of their cleaning service, we also experience the pangs of recession. In a franchise, when challenging times arise, you are still beholden to the franchisor. You might not be able to make all the cost-cutting decisions you would otherwise make if you were on your own, but you also have the support of your franchisor. When times get tough, the franchisor can help you to better manage, market, and maintain your business.

I can't tell you when the next recession will happen, but I can tell you that tomorrow we will be one day closer to it than we are today. As we discussed in the introduction, political control of the government will change, the economy will go up and down, and trends and fads will come and go, but it is up to you to have a positive outlook on your business. It doesn't matter what your personal political leanings are; the guy in the White House, the Speaker of the House, and the Senate Majority Leader have little to do with whether you're successful or not. Don't place blame; instead, stay focused on your goals.

There Are No Guarantees

As I have said, there are no guarantees in life. This is especially true when it comes to business. Because of this, you need to hope for the best but prepare for the worst. I don't mean that in a doom and gloom way, but rather to say that we can't walk into any new business with the expectation that success is guaranteed. What we can do is walk in with a plan and the systems, supports, and drive to execute that plan, knowing those things will likely ensure success. As a franchise owner, you must always be prepared for that one-in-10 risk. That is especially true if you're working in a trendy franchise—whether it's fitness centers or kiosks at the mall. Tastes changes and so do markets. That doesn't mean that those industries aren't worth investing in, but you need to be ahead of the sea change and have a game plan for when that day arrives.

Ultimately, success or failure will all come down to you. If any business isn't successful, we can point our finger at all kinds of reasons—the market we're in, the economy, the franchisor—but we can never control outside circumstances. We can only control ourselves and how we plan and operate our businesses despite the circumstances. As we discussed earlier, you are responsible for the position you are in—not the economy, not the market place, not even the franchisor.

Ask for Help

The most common reason franchises don't succeed is that a franchisee fails to ask for help. You just paid money to not have to reinvent the wheel, so don't try to build a new one when the old one goes flat. If you have a great idea, present it to the franchisor, and see if they agree. Maybe they'll allow you to test it out in your location and perhaps make it a model for the franchise. If not, that's most likely because they have tried it before. Don't get caught up trying to do things your own way. This is why you invested in a franchise.

If you're overwhelmed, please call your franchisor. Almost every time someone calls me with a question or concern, it is almost always one I have confronted myself. We are able to mirror our experiences in order to support one another's success; that is particularly effective with co-franchisees. At Image One, our franchisees have their own relationships. They can call one another to check in and run things past one another. They are able to support each other through their successes, as well as their mistakes. Make sure you choose a franchise with similar supports and be sure to use them.

Tips on Hiring and Firing

Your hiring process may depend on your franchisor, and it will definitely vary depending on the industry and the state in which your franchise operates, but two things will help you in that process: following the franchisor's hiring policies and finding the people who fit. The franchise may have a sample employee handbook for you to use to create your policies and procedures, or they may have one that you are required to use as part of their system.

Remember, just as you searched to find the right fit in a franchisor, so you should search to find the right fit in an employee—not just a fit with you (though that is incredibly important) but also with the community where the store is located, the people and clients you work with, other staff, and any outside vendors with whom the employees will be interacting. You need to hire people who are going to get along with you and the other staff. As I said, you can train for the skills, but you can't change someone's personality.

Also, when it becomes clear the person isn't a fit, there are two things you can do to help yourself: first, if the franchisor has provided termination policies, follow them, and second, don't hold onto the wrong people. It's not always easy to let employees go, but most of the time, the people aren't bad, they're just in the wrong job or at the wrong company. In letting them go, you are freeing them to find a job that is a better fit and freeing yourself to find someone else who is a better fit for your business.

As Jim Collins says in his book, *Good to Great,* you have to make sure you get the right people on the bus and that they're in the right seat. If you find those people and offer them the support they need to succeed, they'll be with you a long time to come.

Patience, Patience, Patience

If franchises ran like engines, the fuel would be patience, though the same is true for most businesses. A lot of people think that things will run more quickly with a franchise. Though it's true that certain processes will be more efficient, as they are already in place, a lot of patience is still necessary to achieve success. Patience with your franchisor, patience with your staff, patience with your customers, and patience with yourself (that might be the hardest one of all) are critical to your success.

Just keep reminding yourself: patience, patience, patience. Now, more than ever, a lack of patience can turn into a customer service nightmare. No matter what you're selling, owning a business means you're in the customer service business. If you make a customer unhappy, that person can write a scathing review that every other potential customer might see; if you make a customer happy, he or she might tell 10 more potential customers.

When I was growing my business, I quickly learned the old adage that the customer is always right. I practiced always keeping my calm no matter how stressful the situation. One day, I was in a heated disagreement with my wife (we've all done that, right?), and I got a call from a client. One minute I was arguing and the next, I was talking to my customer, as calm as could be. When I got off the phone, my wife asked, "Why can't you talk to me like that?"

Ouch. I realized that we have to learn patience everywhere. We have to bring it into our homes, into our work, and into our communities. Patience not only builds success, it makes the world a better place. (As far as patience in my marriage, we are both still working on that after being together over 30 years!)

Have a Good Road Map to Where You Want to Go

Build a grand vision, work hard and smart to make it happen, and ask your franchisor to help you achieve it. Still, you can't ask your franchisor to believe in your vision if you don't have one. Don't needlessly stray from your business plan, and focus your strategies so that you are able to meet the small and large benchmarks along the way.

Once you begin working with your franchisor and you're able to prove your abilities, speak with them to see how they might help you meet those goals—whether it's expanding to more locations, opening in new regions, or growing individual accounts. Write down your five-year goals and see how your franchisor can support you to get there. Figure out what you can start doing today and what choices you need to make in order to reach those goals. If you don't write them down, they're just ideas. Set your deadlines and share with your franchisor where you see yourself in three, five, even 10 years so you can get there together.

When we share our goals with someone else, we are more likely to achieve them. Like writing them down, sharing our goals creates accountability. More than sharing a dream, we are developing a plan to see those goals come true and we're engaging other people in that plan. By sitting down with your franchisor and sharing your road map, you build accountability and partnership towards seeing that vision achieved.

You Are Now a Marketing Expert

So you've got everything running. Things are going well with the franchisor. Business is even beginning to pick up. Now it's time to work harder than ever before because it's now up to you to market your business. Sure, you might receive marketing and advertising support from the franchisor, but you are the face of your business in your community. From industry events to appearances at the Chamber of Commerce, you should be out there networking your business to prospective customers. The success of your business is dependent on the value of your product and on how many people know about it.

A few years ago, I had a franchisee who absolutely refused to market the business. I tried to support him, tried to show him why what he was doing was detrimental to the business, but he believed as long as his services were stellar, he didn't need to spend time marketing them. I'm sure it's no surprise that he's no longer in business.

I tell our franchisees that you need to drop the mop and pick up the iPad. You need to be on social media and out in the community. You need to be connecting with your consumers (and potential consumers) every day. No matter what franchise you choose, you need to go beyond working in the business. You need to always be working on the business to grow it to the next level. That is where you will find your success. You will not find success in mopping a floor or making a sandwich or in repairing a dishwasher. You may make a good living doing those things, but you will not have a successful business if you are the guy on the truck or in the production line of your sandwich shop every day.

You need to be out there in the world, sharing your products and services with the people in your community and those prospective customers who are in need of your product. It's not just about increasing customers (or profit); it's about sharing your experience and value with people in need of both.

We might run a janitorial services franchise, but my real job is Chief Marketing Officer. Every day, I need to be talking about Image One, and our franchisees are no different.

Never slow down on your marketing efforts, even when you first start to taste success. At the same time, make sure you scale your marketing to meet the capabilities of your business. Until you can handle a larger franchise, you have to grow the business strategically. It comes down to striking a balance and making sure that no matter what, you are putting customer service and the customer experience first.

By now, I hope you have gotten a good sense of what it means to become a franchisee. I always tell my franchisees that when you apply enormous amounts of pressure to coal, you get a diamond. The same is true for successful franchises. They take a lot of hard work, pressure, and stamina, but in the end, you can produce a diamond.

Whenever I speak, I always ask people how many of them have bought a treadmill or elliptical. Most people raise their hands. I then ask, "How many of you still use it?" Very few hands stay up. Buying something doesn't always lead to success; if you buy something expecting success but aren't willing to put in the necessary work, you will find yourself going in the opposite direction.

You have to get up every day and maximize your investment to its fullest potential.

If you're looking for a business where you love what you do, are out in the community every day, are able to create flexibility and financial success for you and your family, and can enjoy the benefits of owning your own business without all the risks, I'd say this book has been the right one for you.

If you find the right franchise, you're halfway there. Now, utilize them, collaborate with them, learn from them, and achieve the success that made you want to invest in them in the first place. You can work with the franchise that fits to achieve your biggest goals.

There are no new ideas because the best ones continue to succeed time and time again. By investing in the best idea, you can build a successful business. That work starts today.

And the work continues...

Throughout this book, I have referenced different people and programs that I have been a part of over the years. This is because I am always learning. Even after nearly 35 years in business, I am always learning. This has not only helped me to grow as an entrepreneur and as a business owner, it has also given me a language with which to understand my work, my goals, and the ways in which to achieve and understand success.

Last week I was looking at an evergreen tree on the corner of our home in Illinois. Now, it towers above the roof line, but when I looked at a picture from when we bought the house about 10 years ago, the tree was smaller than the house. Just in the last decade, it has grown an amazing amount, though it wasn't noticeable until I looked at the "then and now" pictures.

A tree will continue to grow until it dies; the same is true for people. It doesn't matter how successful you are or how much you have achieved. In fact, the most successful people are the ones who are always learning and looking for new ways to challenge themselves. We learn as much from our successes as from our mistakes, usually even more from the mistakes. It's like my IRS story: I didn't make a $100,000 mistake, I earned a $100,000 education.

The same goes for you. Never stop growing. Never stop trying. Never stop learning from your mistakes.

Once you get your business up and running, you have just started your education. Now is the time to join the master class. Read more books, meet more people, join a coaching program, a marketing group, a mastermind network, anything you believe will add value to you and your business.

Seeing a dream come true is just the beginning. You need to then keep the dream alive, even when other people say it isn't working, your spouse questions whether you're working too much, and the other side looks a lot greener (and let's face it, a lot easier). In order to keep your new business going, you are going to need to believe in yourself like never before.

If you can stay focused, committed, and inspired, you will begin to see your ROY. Because you have been the one putting in the time and energy, because you have invested your money and experience, now you should begin to see the profits (both financial and emotional) from all your hard work.

I will never forget the first years I saw life-changing profit—the type that helped us buy our first home, made vacations possible, and gave us financial security.

The even greater return was on time.

As a father and a husband, I didn't want to spend my whole life at my job, unavailable to my family. I wanted to be at the game. I wanted to be at practice.

Through my business, I was able to show up for my work but also my family. I was able to create a fulfilled life. Today, as a franchisor, I get to watch the same return for my franchisees as well as my sons. I watch as people leave independent businesses or W2 jobs to discover what it means to run a successful business that also offers them flexibility and support.

Running a successful business is 80% hard work and 20% luck, but the more you work and the more you learn, the more luck you will have. When luck comes my way, I take advantage of it! Focus on abundance, and you will find that things are abundant; focus on scarcity, and you will find yourself in a scarce world.

If you're still afraid to make the leap, ask yourself: what is stopping me?

If it's just a matter of not being interested in franchising, no problem. It was nice getting to spend some time with you and congrats on making it to the end of the book.

But if you're interested in opening a franchise, if you feel you could be successful, if you have a sense of what you want to do, today is the day to do it. To quote Dan Sullivan again, "Ask who, not how!"

Most entrepreneurs encounter problems and ask themselves, "How am I going to do this?" The question, however, isn't how; it's who. Who is going to help me solve this problem? Today you are looking for a business opportunity. The who may just be the franchisor that is right in front of you. Figure out who (which franchise) will best serve your needs, and go for it!

We all have a unique ability. Now is the time to discover yours, and to employ it in making your grand vision come true. You can do that in a number of different ways, but if franchising is your way, now is the time to get out there and start learning.

I hope this book has provided you with a solid foundation.

If you are looking for more information, you can go to our website at www.TimsFranchiseBook.com.

If you've ever looked at your life and thought, "Wow, I thought I'd be further along by now," don't let another opportunity pass you by! Tomorrow is not the time to start, because there will always be another tomorrow. There is only one today. If you know where you want to go, if you're looking for a significant ROY, franchising can offer you more than just profit and flexibility. It can offer you fulfillment.

And the opportunity to never go on a job interview again.

Acknowledgements

Thanks to a great team and to our franchisees! Without the team in the office and the franchisees they support, there would be no business. Having such an amazing team has given me the freedom to develop the vision you all work so hard to make a reality. Your hard work is what makes Image One shine!

Thank you to Mike, my business partner of almost 20 years and co-founder of Image One. If not for our partnership, I would likely still be running an independent janitorial company without ever having considered the possibility of franchising.

Special thanks to Anna David and Kristen McGuiness; without both of you, your ideas, and your guidance, this book would not be what it is. Thank you for making the process such a wonderful experience. I can't thank you enough! I already have my next book in mind...

About the Author

 Tim Conn started his first small business at the age of 14, cleaning a small office building that his parents owned. He operated Tidy Tim's Cleaning Service from 1985-2001 before launching into the wild world of franchises.

In 2011, he and his partner Mike Schuchman founded Image One, a franchised cleaning service company that has revolutionized the industry. He enjoys spending time with Maria, his wife of 26 years and their two sons Anthony and Nikko, who are both franchise owners in his business.

For more information about franchises, visit www.TimsFranchiseBook.com.